OUT OF THE DARKroom

A Short History of the Photofinishing Industry

By

Peter L M Rockwell and Peter W Knaack

www.2ppress.com

Published in Great Britain in 2006 by
2 P Press
7A Courthouse Road
London N12 7PH, UK
+44 20 8445 3574
info@2ppress

ISBN 978-0-9554072-0-8
ISBN 0-99554072-0-6

Copy Editing Linda Bristow – Devon, UK

Design by Pamela Kende ELA Design Ltd
630 Monroe River Forest, IL 60305 Tel: 708-366-6780
ELA_Design@comcast,net

Cover by Benjamin Kende Photography
2118 W. Superior St. Chicago, IL 60612
www.kendephotography.com benny@kendephotography.com
Tel: 773-278-7723 Fax: 773-278-7782

The text of this book is set in Garamond and Century Gothic.

To our wives

Eva and Gudrun

OUT OF THE DARKroom

A Short History
of the Photofinishing Industry

Contents

An Apology to Our Readers.

Photography and photofinishing has been a global industry longer than most and we know no way of writing a book in English using spelling and phrases to suit every taste. For the last 40 years we have managed to communicate with English speakers from all over the world without too many misunderstandings and so we ask you to accept the language we learnt in Europe, together with a few expressions we acquired in our travels round the world.

Preface

Ask any one of the hundreds of millions of families in the affluent industrial world what they have in common with their peers and after a moment of contemplation, they will come up with a list of worldly goods including a camera and albums or boxes of photos recording the life of their families. Behind that pastime of photography lies photofinishing, a fascinating industry.

In 1886 George Eastman coined the famous slogan "You press the button – we do the rest". The rest, that is the developing and printing of films, was the start of the photofinishing industry. An essential part of amateur photography, although not widely known, it was for many years a cottage industry carried out by hundreds of thousands of photo shops, but in the second half of the 20th century, it became a major industry worldwide.

For most people the interval between sending the film to be developed and receiving the prints is somewhat of a mystery. For many years, developing and printing was literally carried out in the dark, but that is no longer so. The growth of picture taking, accompanied by the rise and subsequent transformation of the photofinishing industry during the last 50 years is a fascinating story.

Until after the Second World War, the majority of pictures taken were black and white. From the fifties onwards there was a gradual shift towards colour; initially transparencies and later prints, so that by the Millennium the overwhelming majority of the output of the industry were colour prints.

The size and growth of the industry was primarily governed by the sales of cameras and films and very little influenced by the marketing efforts of the photofinishers. For many years there was a rapid growth in photography, so that there was more than enough for anyone capable of offering the service. Like many other profitable industries, it has since become very competitive and everybody is fighting hard either to obtain or retain their share.

A good indication of the scale of the industry is that in the United States, the largest market, almost 1 billion films were sold in the year 2000. Add to that the fact that the cost of developing and printing is usually higher than the cost of the films and it is soon apparent why photofinishing has been the significant part of the photographic industry which has been eagerly fought over by the major players such as Kodak and Fuji.

In the last few years the industry has changed dramatically as picture taking has changed from film to digital cameras. Many well known names have come and gone and some new ones have taken their place. The era of having one's films "developed and printed" is coming to an end and it seems likely that, before the end of the first decade of this century, film may well be a rarity. There are now many options for dealing with one's pictorial memories and this account tells how these have evolved over the last 120 years.

CHAPTER 1

A Brief History of Photography to 1950

It is surprising that photography was not invented until the mid 19th century. The two ingredients of photography: namely, producing an image and the technology behind the method of reproducing that image, had been known for several centuries, but had never been combined to produce what we now call a photograph. The word itself, which is based on the Greek words for light and drawing, was coined by Sir John Herschel in 1839.

For several hundred years it was known that silver nitrate and silver chloride blackened with time, but no one was sure why. In 1727 Professor Schulze, of the University of Altdorf, heated some silver nitrate in an oven and noticed that it did not blacken. So he decided to eliminate the effect of heat altogether. When he made up a mixture of chalk, nitric acid and silver in a flask, he noticed a darkening of the solution which was facing the sun. [1 2] He then had the idea of covering the side of the flask with various templates and made the remarkable discovery of what is fundamental to all photography as we now know it. Where the template covered the flask he observed a white image had formed in the solution. However, the image continued to blacken as at that time there was no known way of "fixing" it.

Tracing photography to its origins, the camera obscura, which allows images to be projected on a wall in a darkened room, had been in existence since the middle ages; Leonardo Da Vinci had sketched it in 1519. It was then improved in the 17th century by fitting a telescope lens instead of a pinhole and subsequently portable versions were used by artists to project an image onto a screen as an aid to drawing. So here was something not far removed from today's cameras. All that was needed was a "film".

The Beginning

The real breakthrough came in the following century. In 1839 Louis Daguerre in France and then shortly afterwards, Henry Fox Talbot in England, announced the results of a series of experiments which they had been conducting over many years.

Daguerre produced superb images on a metal plate, which was covered with a thin layer of silver. The silver was made light sensitive by treating it with iodine and bromine vapour, which formed a thin layer of silver iodide and silver bromide. The freshly sensitised plates were then exposed in the camera, often for as much as half an hour. This produced only a barely visible image, which was then developed by placing the plate in an atmosphere of mercury vapour. After a few minutes an enhanced image of silver amalgam appeared. Finally, the image was fixed by placing the plate in sodium thiosulphate, commonly called hypo, which removes the remaining silver iodide and bromide.[3]

The French government bought the rights to the process and made it freely available, which helped to make it very popular. The results were superb and the process caused a sensation and many of the so-called Daguerreotypes, which were produced at the time, are still in existence today. However, it did have one major disadvantage: that only a single image could be reproduced from each exposure.

A few weeks after Daguerre had made his announcement in Paris, Fox Talbot in London published his process, which was the first to utilise a negative exposed while inside the camera. The negative was made by brushing a sheet of paper with a weak salt solution, followed by a weak silver nitrate solution, creating a thin coating of light-sensitive silver chloride. The negatives produced in this way were not very sensitive and required long exposures of as much as half an hour. The paper negatives, with their black silver images, were then fixed by treating with Hypo, which dissolved the remaining silver chloride. This part of the process had been discovered a few years earlier, by Fox Talbot's friend Sir John Herschel.

The prints were made by placing the negative on top of another sheet of paper and then exposing them to sunlight. By this means, taking the process one step further than Daguerre had done, any number of prints could be made from one negative.

In the following year Fox Talbot made some improvements to his process, increasing the sensitivity, so that exposures of less than half a minute were sufficient to produce an image. He named this the Calotype process. The quality of Calotypes was not as good as that of Daguerreotypes, but paper prints were more convenient and much less expensive. One of the limitations of the Calotypes was that prints exposed through paper negatives were not very sharp and showed the texture of the paper. To make things worse, Fox Talbot had patented his process and was reluctant to grant licences, other than to amateurs, and this held back his process compared to Daguerreotypes.

Glass Plates

A few years later, Frederick Scott Archer took a big step forward, by introducing what he called the Collodion process, in which the negative was on a glass plate. The difficulty in using glass for the base of the negative was how to find a way of spreading the light-sensitive substances uniformly and making them adhere to the glass plate. This required a binder, which in this case was a viscous liquid consisting of guncotton dissolved in ether and alcohol.

Collodion negatives were sharper and showed much more detail than Calotypes. What is more, they were much more sensitive, requiring exposures of only 1 or 2 seconds, thus making it possible to take portraits and other similar subjects. Their main drawback was that the plates lost their sensitivity when dry, so they had to be coated, exposed and processed while still wet. Despite this complication they were in use for over 20 years.

The next breakthrough was made by Dr. Richard Maddox, who was an English physician and great photo enthusiast. He was prompted to refine the Collodion process due to the fact that the ether used in the Collodion process affected his health. In 1871 he proposed that the light-sensitive chemicals could be coated onto a glass plate in a gelatine emulsion. One big feature of this method was that these worked when dry and could be kept for a period of time without deterioration, which meant that the plates no longer had to be produced by the photographer. Several people worked on this idea and a few years later Charles Bennett was the first to market dry plates. By 1880 there were a large number of manufacturers of dry plates in several countries and the Collodion wet-plate process had been completely replaced. During this part of the of the late 19th century, many photographic studios sprang up, some producing Daguerreotypes, others Collotypes, followed by a rush to use dry plates. In fact most of the major towns of England, France, Germany and the US had studios. There were particularly large concentrations of these in London, Paris, Berlin and New York. In addition, there were many scientific and amateur photographers. Until 1880, photographers had to make and develop their own plates because materials, which were ready to expose, did not exist and there was nowhere to have them developed and printed.

At this time photographic emulsions were only sensitive to blue and violet light, which meant that green and red objects appeared to be very dark. In 1873 Herman Vogel, a German chemist, discovered that adding certain dyes to the emulsions would make them sensitive to green light as well as to blue and violet. These orthochromatic plates, sensitive to all visible light, except red and deep orange, gave a much more realistic result.[4] At the turn of the century "panchromatic" plates, which were sensitive to the whole of the visible spectrum, followed. This ability to adjust the spectral sensitivity of photographic emulsions is one of the key technologies of colour photography.

There had been a number of attempts to produce coloured images, but, except for hand-coloured photographs, which became quite popular, nothing practical emerged.

Colour Photography Demonstration

Back in May 1861 James Clerk Maxwell, a physicist better known for his work on electromagnetism, had demonstrated what would later become the basis of colour photography. He prepared three slides of a coloured ribbon, exposed respectively through red, green and blue filters. He set up three magic lanterns, the name by which slide projectors were known in those days, and projected the three slides through the same red, green and blue filters that had been used when they were prepared. The three projected images thus formed were carefully superimposed and the result was a colour image of the ribbon. We shall see later how colour photography, even to this day, uses this combination of three images each exposed to part of the visible light spectrum.

Ilford

After 1880, when dry plates became available from an increasing number of manufacturers, photography grew rapidly and we had the beginnings of a major industry. Some of the names which are common today had begun to emerge. In 1879, Alfred Harman, who had operated several studios in London, decided to give up photography and concentrate on manufacturing dry plates. He founded the Britannia Works, which grew rapidly and in 1901 was renamed Ilford, after the town on the east side of London, where it was based.[5]

George Eastman – The Father of Snap-shooting

The person of far greater significance to the photographic industry was George Eastman. In 1868, at the age of 14, to help support his widowed mother and two sisters, he started work as a messenger on $3 a week. Being very ambitious, he taught himself book-keeping, so that by the age of 20, he had become a bank clerk, earning $15, and was able to indulge in what was to become his passion: photography. He acquired the equipment and materials for the wet plate process, but found it too complicated, particularly as he wanted to take pictures while travelling. He read in the British Journal of Photography about the dry plate processes of Dr. Richard Maddox and Charles Bennett and decided that would be the way forward. Working in his mother's kitchen, he developed his own process and possibly more importantly, designed a machine for coating the emulsion onto the glass plates. In 1879, aged 25, he travelled to London, which was then the centre of photography, to register a patent for his plate-coating machine and to obtain the latest recipes.[6]

On his return, he started to manufacture dry plates, while still working at the bank. The business was successful, but needed more capital. In January 1881 he went into partnership with Henry A Strong, a buggy whip manufacturer, who had lodged with his mother. They formed the Eastman Dry Plate Company and soon had six employees. Shortly afterwards Eastman gave up his job with the bank, to devote all his efforts to his new business.

George Eastman was a remarkable man, characterised by his energy, vision and sheer ability. His ambition was to make photography an activity that everybody could afford and master, rather than something which was only available to highly skilled professionals and enthusiastic amateurs. He quickly realised that he had to provide the complete system, rather than just the plates. Unlike many other pioneers, he was not afraid to seek help, and from the very beginning, he engaged the most talented people he could find to develop his ideas.

He hit on the idea of putting the emulsion on a flexible support, which could be rolled up, rather than on a glass plate. His first "film" as it was called, consisted of an emulsion coated on a strip of paper. With the assistance of William Walker, he produced a roll holder that would fit in the place of the glass plate of the current cameras. There were problems with printing the negatives, as the paper base was not as transparent as a glass plate. Eastman came up with a neat solution: after development, he stripped the emulsion from the paper and transferred it to a transparent base for contact printing. This worked very well, but proved to be time consuming. The roll films in their holders were a success; however Eastman's prediction that they would completely replace glass plates was not borne out. He decided that he would have to do something dramatically different to popularise photography.

He next engaged Henry Reichenbach, a chemist, to improve the film. Together they developed a transparent nitro-cellulose base on which the emulsion could be coated. Initially the film was made on long glass tables, onto which the film base was cast. After it had dried and hardened, the photographic emulsion was cast on top. Finally the film was slit into strips. In 1889, only four months after they had gone into production, Reichenbach was granted a patent for this method of producing roll films.

The next step was to design a camera, which could be produced in large numbers at an affordable price. Eastman was one of the first manufacturers to set up for mass production by designing a camera made of interchangeable parts. This dramatically reduced the time it took to build and hence the cost of the cameras. Eastman caused a sensation when, in 1888, he launched the $25 "Kodak" camera loaded with enough film for 100 exposures. The launch was accompanied by the famous slogan

"You press the button we do the rest". The customer would return the camera with the exposed film to Eastman Kodak, as the company was now called and for $10 would receive back a set of prints and the camera loaded with fresh film. This was the beginning of the photofinishing industry as we know it today.

Eastman, a great marketer, was looking for a name for his products, which would be easy to publicise, and in 1888 registered the name "Kodak" as a trademark. It was an invented word. The letter "K" was his favourite and he experimented with various combinations beginning and ending with K and came up with the famous name. [7]

One can only speculate as to whether he realised how valuable a brand it would become in later years. He advertised his cameras extensively, the aim being to spread his products round the world. His first overseas office opened in London in 1885, followed by his first overseas manufacturing plant in Harrow, England, in 1891.

In 1890 Eastman launched his first daylight-loading camera, using a film with a black paper backing to keep out the light. During the next few years he launched a succession of cameras, including folding models, heralding the age of the portable camera.

The really big step towards the popularisation of photography came in 1900, when Eastman launched the first Brownie camera. At only $1 for the camera, plus 15 cents for the film, many more people could afford photography and this sparked the creation of one of the most popular pastimes. The cameras were produced in vast numbers. Successive models, of both the box and folding type, were in production for almost 70 years.

Brownie Junior Camera

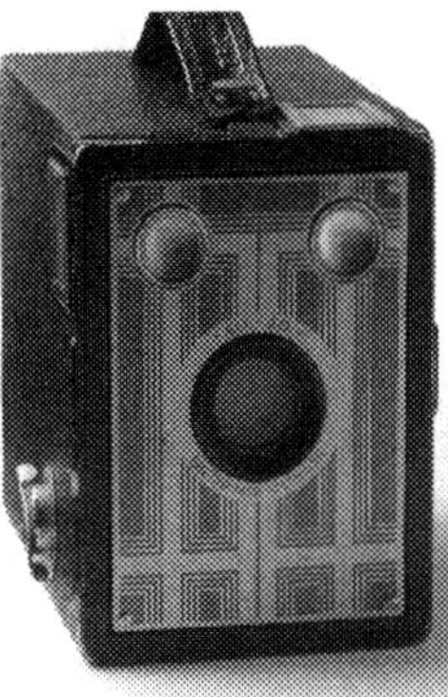

To realise his ambitious plans, Eastman actively built up all parts of the business. He was one of the first in the photographic industry to start a dedicated research department recruiting the most able people he could find, several of whom were from overseas. He focused on designing machinery to improve the quality and reduce the cost of his products and bought up competitors for their expertise and patents. At an early stage he set out to control his essential raw materials, such as gelatine, paper and film base. Marketing and advertising were never far from his thoughts. The growth was phenomenal: by 1907 Kodak was employing more than 5,000 people world-wide.

Eastman and his staff registered many patents. An interesting case is that of the roll film, of which Eastman is credited as being the originator. That was not strictly true, although he was certainly the first to manufacture them in quantity. In 1887 the Reverend Hanibal Goodwin of Newark, New Jersey, who had experimented with photography, applied for and was granted a patent for roll film. He was unable to raise sufficient funds to go into production himself, however, as the rightful patent owner, in 1889 he filed a patent infringement case against Eastman, which rumbled on in the courts for many years. Goodwin never personally benefited from his patent having died the following year as a result of a streetcar accident. However, in 1914, a court ordered Eastman to pay Ansco, the subsequent holder of Goodwin's patent, $5 million in damages for infringement. The size of the award gives some indication of the scale of Kodak's business, taking into account the low cost of the films.

Cine

Another milestone was reached in 1889. Thomas Edison was trying to develop cinematography and he decided to use film made by Eastman. The Eastman film in use at the time was 70 mm wide, but Edison ordered a strip half that width and that is how the 35mm format came into being. He punched perforations into the edge of the film and these have remained unchanged to this day. Its subsequent use for still photography had to wait for a few more years. Several years later, the Lumiere brothers from Lyon, France, adopted the same width for their cine film, although initially they used different perforations.

By the start of the 20th century, practical photography had been known for over 50 years and had blossomed in England, France, the United States and Germany. There were large numbers of professional photographers taking portraits, as well as serious amateurs, many of whom were astronomers or scientists from other disciplines. We are here defining professionals as those for whom photography was a livelihood, as opposed to those for whom it was either a hobby or an adjunct to other interests.

For most of this period, photographers had to make their own materials to produce Daguerreotypes or Collodion prints or variants of these. It was only towards the end of the 19th century that ready-sensitised dry plates could be bought. However, even these had to be developed and printed by the photographer, which was far from straightforward. The production of dry plates was a relatively simple process and by the end of the century there were small companies all over the world producing them. The total number of dry plates in production must have been considerable, as by 1890 several manufacturers were hand coating 12,000 plates per day and others were using machines which produced similar quantities.[8] The plates were quite large and were often cut into smaller sizes, further increasing the number of plates. This is the origin of the whole, half and quarter plate sizes. As more people got in on the act, it became a very competitive industry.

It is worth considering the two companies founded before the start of the 20th century, both very different in character, but both of which were still very much up and running 100 years later. Ilford, founded in 1879, claimed only twelve years later to be the largest manufacturer of plates in the world. This may have been the case, although the French company Lumiere might have disputed that claim. Ilford's founder was fairly conservative in outlook and despite having had considerable success in producing dry plates and printing paper, decided not to proceed with "rollable" films, as his initial trials were not very successful. In fact it was not until well into the 1920s that Ilford started manufacturing roll films, having previously concentrated on improving the quality of their plates and thereby establishing their reputation with professional photographers.

George Eastman, or Eastman Kodak as his company was called from 1892, was quite the opposite. Having started with dry plates, Eastman did not want to spend his life competing with the rest of the industry on price. As soon as he had mastered the art of producing "rollable" films he concentrated all his efforts on these, together with the cameras and processing. It was an extremely courageous move: the quality of early films did not match that of plates, so that many of the established photographers of the time showed little interest in them. Films and Brownie cameras in particular, were aimed at a completely different, but eventually much larger, market. Kodak, through mass production and very aggressive marketing, managed to create a new pastime and establish an enormous lead over everyone else. There was virtually no competition in the snap-shooter market for a long time and it was 20 or more years before any of the other major players started to produce roll films.

Agfa, part of the German chemical company Bayer, started producing developers in 1873, but it was not until 1912 that the company built a factory in Leverkusen to manufacture film, chemicals and paper. In a similar way, the Italian company

Ferrania started to produce nitro-cellulose mixture in 1915, but its first film and paper products were not released until 1927.[9]

In Japan, Konica's origins date from the middle of the 19th century. However, it was not until 1903 that they produced the first photo papers. Sakura, as Konica's films were then called, were not released until 1929. Fuji started film production even later.

This is not to say that in 1900 there were no film producers other than Kodak. There must have been countless examples around the world. For instance, Birt Acres, an English pioneer of cine cameras, in 1894 produced his own 35 mm film stock in North London, shortly afterwards adopting what were known as the Edison perforations. However, he soon abandoned film manufacture, as he found he was able to purchase much better and less expensive film from Kodak. [10] Manufacturers such as these were of no long-term consequence, especially as Eastman made sure quite early on that his products were available world wide at competitive prices. In addition to the factories in Rochester and Harrow, Kodak opened offices in Paris, Toronto and several other cities around the world. It was not very long before he started to manufacture in Paris and Australia.

In contrast, by 1900 there were many companies producing cameras. Most were plate cameras and it was not until Kodak films were well established, that companies in France, Germany, England and of course the US, many of them in Rochester, started manufacturing roll film cameras.

Eastman, never one to welcome competition, bought up as many dry plate and camera manufacturers as he could. In 1897, and again in 1902, he made attempts to merge with or take over Ilford, but without success. The comparative figures for the two companies at the time of the second bid show the enormous strides Kodak had made: Eastman Kodak had an issued share capital of $24 million and in the second half of 1902 had made a profit of $1.5 million, whereas Ilford's capital was $1.9 million and its profit for the whole of that year was $257,500. (Exchange rate £1 = $5).[11] So, by the turn of the century, Kodak was already ten times the size of its nearest competitor. This kind of dominance over other photographic companies prevailed for nearly three-quarters of a century, despite several attempts by the anti-trust authorities in the US and Europe to encourage competition.

Eastman's first brush with the anti-trust authorities was in 1915, when the district court found that Kodak had monopolised the amateur camera, film, and photofinishing industries by means of acquisitions and a variety of exclusionary practices. [12] Kodak tried to fight the ruling, but after six years abandoned its appeal. In 1921, Kodak entered a consent decree with the US government, in force for over 70 years, whereby it disposed of some of its acquisitions and agreed not to produce private label films. The purpose of this was to prevent Kodak marketing "fighting" brands designed to drive its competitors out of the market. As a result of this policy, for many years all of its products were marked as manufactured by Kodak.

Roll films in the early 1900s had several limitations, which meant that they were not used by professionals or by serious enthusiasts. Prints were generally produced by contact and this limited their size to 3 ½"x 2 ½" (6 x 9 cm). Professionals, on the other hand, could use large glass plates and so portraits of a considerable size were not a problem. Most contact printing was done using natural light and this was one reason why many studios had rooms which received northern light.

Picture enlargement had not really been established as a process; for one thing the printing papers were not very sensitive, which would have meant very long exposures, a highly dangerous procedure with the inflammable cellulose nitrate negatives of the time. This was also a serious problem in the early years of the cinema, until the cellulose acetate safety film base was introduced in 1908. Another factor was that emulsions frequently had pinholes, a much more serious situation with enlarged images. Furthermore, the film base was not as stable as glass and this was another reason for professionals to shun it. It took many years and considerable improvements for professionals to be won over to film.

A considerable part of Eastman's success was that he provided not only the films and cameras for snapshooters, but that he also set up the developing services. These were situated initially in Rochester and Harrow, but other facilities followed shortly afterwards in England, France, Germany and Hungary.[13]

After daylight loadable, paper-backed film was introduced in 1891, the cameras no longer needed to be sent back to Rochester or Harrow. This enabled others to process amateur films and thus cleared the way for independent developing and printing (D&P) services, which are now called photofinishing.

Since the early part of the 20th century there has been a steady improvement in the quality of photographic materials. Eastman had set up a major research lab in Rochester followed by one in Harrow. These studied not only the emulsions, but also the manufacturing technology, especially film and paper coating. This had a considerable influence on improving uniformity, eliminating pin holes and of course ultimately reducing the cost of production. From the twenties, other manufacturers such as Ilford, Agfa, Ferrania and Ansco were also busy making amateur films and this spur of competition led to improved film quality.

In parallel with the improvements in sensitised materials there was frenetic development of cameras. By 1920 Kodak had launched over 125 models, notwithstanding the fact that some were on the market for a short time only. They ranged in price from $1 for the first Brownie to $109.50. However, a good proportion cost less than $10, a reflection of how Kodak had always tried to encourage photography by producing relatively inexpensive cameras. Not all were roll film cameras as Kodak was still active in the professional market. In the period up to 1920 they introduced about 35 different models of cameras for use with glass plates, but, interestingly, no more after that year.[14]

Kodak was not the only one active in camera manufacture. As photography spread, independent camera manufacturers sprang up all over the world. There were many plate cameras, usually built of wood with ornate brass fittings. As the quality of films improved, a number of companies started producing both fixed and folding cameras. The low cost of Kodak cameras encouraged many of the independents to produce more up-market models. Names such as Graphlex, Ensign, Agfa, Zeiss, Ikon, Leitz and Rolleiflex became well known in the 1920s and 30s. This in turn stimulated the lens manufacturers who produced a succession of better optics. Companies including Bausch & Lomb, Bell & Howell, Schneider, Rodenstock, Leitz, Zeiss, Dallmeyer, Ross and Taylor Hobson, who had previously been producing microscopes or telescopes, became known for their camera lenses.

The Leica

A major development in photography was the use of 35mm film for still photography. The idea was quite revolutionary as, at that time, nearly all photographs were made by contact printing and that involved large negatives. In 1912, Oskar Barnack, a keen photographer who had trained as a machinist before working as a designer at Leitz, had become frustrated at the heavy weight of so-called portable cameras. While experimenting with a cine camera, he wondered why, since it was possible to project a large image onto a screen from a small transparency, it would not be possible to make prints from similarly small negatives.

Barnack built a very compact camera that used 35 mm cine film, but by turning the image on the film through 90ª, he arranged to produce a negative 24 mm x 36 mm, which was twice the size of a cine frame. The results were excellent and almost certainly better than those obtained with roll-film cameras. There were good reasons for this. Barnack was a brilliant mechanic, so was able to produce a much more precise camera than was usual at the time, and he combined it with an excellent Leitz lens. He built a second prototype and carried out extensive tests. However, progress was halted by the outbreak of World War 1.

After the war, due to the chaotic economic conditions in Germany, the project lay dormant for several years. Finally Leitz decided to revive it and, in 1925, the Leica (**LEI**tz **CA**mera) was launched. Initial reactions were mixed. Many of the professionals, who were still using glass plates, did not take it seriously, while others, who appreciated its high quality and portability, took to it with enthusiasm. In the following few years, several other manufacturers which were centred around Germany, started manufacturing 35 mm cameras, so that by the late 1930s it was a well established format, especially amongst serious enthusiasts and journalists.

Practical Colour Photography

There had been many attempts to produce colour processes since Maxwell, but most had limited success. One of the notable exceptions must surely be the Autochrome process patented in 1903 by the Lumiere brothers of Lyon, France, who in 1895 had been amongst the pioneers of cinematography. It was the first practical colour photographic process. Autochrome plates consisted of a glass plate covered with a mixture of tiny starch globules, which had been dyed blue, green and red. These globules were fixed to the glass using a clear lacquer. A photographic emulsion was then coated over the layer of coloured globules. The plate was exposed in the camera through the starch globules, which acted as colour filters, and was then developed as a transparency.

The results were impressive. Between 1907 and 1930, many millions of Autochrome plates were produced. Their complexity and the fact that they could not easily be projected or printed, meant that their use was confined to very serious enthusiasts.

Another notable process of the period was known as Dufaycolor. In principle, it was similar to Autochrome, in which a black and white image was produced and viewed through three sets of colour filters. The difference lay in the way the filters were produced. Dufaycolor, which was coated on a film base, had a filter mosaic consisting of very narrow lines running at angles to each other. The three sets of lines were respectively dyed blue, green and red, forming filters through which the exposures were made and viewed. One feature, important at the time, was that the transparencies could be projected and copied. [15]

Between 1908 and 1932 Dufaycolor went through various incarnations in France after which it passed into the hands of Spicers, the UK papermaker and then in 1935 it was taken over by Ilford. For several years they produced both cine and 120 size roll films for amateurs. Ilford's production of Dufaycolor was fairly short-lived, as much better processes became available shortly afterwards. The reason that it merits a mention here is that, for a few years in the early thirties, it was unique in that it allowed an amateur photographer to pop a roll of film into his camera, send the exposed film to Ilford and then receive back a colour transparency.

Autochrome and Dufaycolor were the most successful of what are termed additive processes. Additive processes take three images, which are the blue, green and red components of the scene and combine these to create a colour picture. Doing this on a single film or sheet of paper has some fairly severe limitations. If you superimpose a blue, green and red filter, no light will pass through. The alternative is to do what Autochrome and Dufaycolor did and place the three filters side by side. To get satisfactory definition, these filter elements must be very small. With each colour only occupying one-third of the image area, the sensitivity of the film is reduced and the brightness of the print or transparency is heavily restricted.

The converse of this is what is termed a subtractive process, where the three images are superimposed on each other. It is not possible to do this with blue, green and red images, but it can be done with images of the complementary colours, yellow, magenta and cyan.

From the early thirties, a number of processes appeared for making colour transparencies or prints by taking three images through blue, green and red filters and then, after development, dying them yellow, magenta and cyan. The three coloured images were then superimposed.

All modern photographic processes are like this, but the method of achieving it varies considerably. The only additive colour systems still in regular use are television and computer displays.

The idea of producing a film or print with yellow, magenta and cyan images superimposed, was a daunting task. One of the first to do this successfully was Technicolor, who in 1932 launched what was the fourth and final version of their cine process. It used a specially built camera, which split the image into three parts and exposed three films simultaneously through blue, green and red filters. The three films then went through a fairly complicated process to produce yellow, magenta and cyan images, which were then superimposed. The system was very complicated both in terms of the camera taking three films simultaneously and also the processing which, while successful for the cinema, was impractical for the still photographer.

From the beginning of the 20th century people had been experimenting and registering patents for films which would expose all three images on a single film, but it was not until about 1930 that any met with success. The basic idea was to coat three photographic emulsions on top of each other and make each one sensitive to a different part of the visible spectrum. Sensitising dyes had been known for a long time, but the choice of dyes was very limited. There was no way in which an emulsion could be produced that was only sensitive to one part of the spectrum. The other problem was that, if several photographic emulsions were coated one on top of another, they invariably reacted with one another.

The breakthrough was finally made by two friends, by the name of Leopold Mannes and Leopold Godowsky, who were both very keen photographers and very talented musicians. For a long time they could not make up their minds which career to pursue. From the early 1920s they earned their living as a pianist and a violinist and in their spare time experimented in their parents' home with various colour processes. In 1922 they were introduced to Dr. Mees, Eastman Kodak's research director. Kodak had been working on colour processes for many years, but had not come up with anything particularly promising. Dr. Mees liked what they were doing and offered to assist them by providing them with specially coated plates. On the strength of Kodak's assistance they were able to raise a substantial loan and set up a small laboratory in a New York hotel room.

By the late 1920s, Kodak had made some advances in sensitising dyes and this, combined with Mannes' and Godowsky's work, looked as if it could be the basis of a practical colour process. At the end of 1930 they joined Kodak, moving to Rochester shortly after that. In April 1935 Kodak announced the new process, called Kodachrome, and this was undoubtedly Kodak's first step to world leadership in colour photography.

The five-layer Kodachrome film consisted of three photographic emulsions, sensitised to different parts of the spectrum and interspersed with two clear gelatine layers to reduce interaction between the photographic emulsions. The top layer, which was blue-sensitive was coloured with a yellow dye* to stop the blue light from affecting either of the two lower layers. Sensitising dyes which would make the film sensitive to only one part of the spectrum did not exist, so the lower layers were sensitised to blue and green light and to blue and red light. Combined with the yellow filter, the effect of this arrangement was that we have a film with three superimposed black and white emulsions, sensitive respectively, to blue, green and red light. At this stage it was still a far cry from what we now know as a colour film.

The clever part of Mannes' and Godowsky's work was to design a process whereby the three superimposed layers could be developed and then selectively dyed yellow, magenta and cyan, thus forming a colour image. The process was and is extremely complicated, initially involving 28 steps and taking 3½ hours to complete.

**A yellow filter will block blue light, but permit the remainder of the visible spectrum, particularly green and red light, to pass.*

Consequently for almost 20 years, Kodak carried out all processing themselves. Kodachrome films were sold process paid, which was of considerable benefit to Kodak, as the relatively simple B&W film was not difficult to produce: most of the complication and cost lay in the process. Kodak's patents prevented other manufacturers from producing similar films until after World War Two.

Kodachrome was launched as 16mm, followed shortly afterwards by 8mm cine film. 35mm still camera film was not released until the end of 1936, probably because 35mm film and cameras were not very widespread outside Europe. Initially, the processed films were returned as uncut rolls and could be viewed against a light or wound through a projector, which not many people had at the time. A big advance occurred in 1939 when Kodak returned the films mounted in cardboard slide mounts ready for projection. It was probably one of the factors which popularised 35mm photography and stimulated a number of companies to produce low-cost 35mm cameras.

Kodachrome was a major breakthrough and set the standard as far as colour transparency film was concerned. Ilford discontinued Dufaycolor and no other serious contenders emerged to produce additive colour processes.

Kodachrome produced superb results. However, the serious disadvantage was that the processing was very complicated and this ruled out using it for producing prints from amateur snapshots. What was needed, was a film that produced colour prints using a simple process. Because of the limitations of additive processes, such as Dufaycolor, what was required was a film with three layers respectively sensitive to blue, green and red light, producing yellow, magenta and cyan images. This meant correctly sensitised emulsions, but also incorporating dyestuffs, which after processing, would form the coloured images.

Both Kodak and Agfa, amongst others, had succeeded in producing single layer coloured images sensitised to different parts of the visible spectrum. The emulsions incorporated substances, called colour couplers, which form either a yellow, magenta or cyan image when the silver halide image is developed. The remaining silver could then be removed, leaving only the colour image. However, for a long time neither company could produce multilayer coatings of different colours, because of the interaction between the various sensitizers and colour couplers .

This problem was first solved by Agfa, who selected a particular sized molecular structure of the silver halides which were used in the emulsions. This eliminated, or in any case sufficiently reduced the diffusion of dyestuffs between layers, resulting in a multilayer film with incorporated colour couplers.

In 1936, Agfa released a colour transparency film and, shortly afterwards, colour negative film for movies; colour paper followed later. The first public presentation of paper prints was rumoured to have taken place in 1942, but due to the war was not launched until about 1950.

The processing of the Agfa materials was much simpler than Kodachrome. Agfa set up processing labs for the reversal material in Berlin, Prague and Vienna and it also became available in the UK in the summer of 1939. The price of a 36 exposure cassette was £0.30, equivalent nowadays to about $1.20.

Agfa–Ansco, the US associates of Agfa, introduced Anscocolor, their version of the reversal film in 1938, but production ceased with the outbreak of the war in 1939. Production restarted after the company was taken over by the US Government in 1942, but during the war years the films were produced for military use only.

After the war, parties of British and American scientists visited the Agfa factories in Wolfen and Leverkusen and issued reports on the formulae and production methods of Agfa materials. These were made freely available to anyone who requested them. As a result, a number of companies, including GAF in the US, ICI and Pakolor in the UK, Ferrania in Italy, Valca in Spain, Telko in Switzerland and Fuji, Konishiroku and Oriental in Japan, started the production of films based on the Agfa processes. Most were transparency films, but some eventually produced colour negative films and printing papers. The results were rather variable and some made only a brief appearance on the market.

Eastman Kodak at one time considered marketing Kodachrome roll film and prints but the processing was far too complicated. They had, however, developed a similar negative film to Agfa, but solved the problem of interaction between the layers in a different way. Kodacolor, as the negative/positive print process was called, encapsulated the colour couplers in an oily emulsion, which stopped them migrating from layer to layer.

Kodacolor was launched in the US in early 1942. The films had to be taken to a retailer and sent back to Rochester for processing, as Kodak did not supply chemicals or details of the process. Although the chemical process was considerably simpler than that required for Kodachrome transparencies, making colour prints was still very difficult and Kodak believed, and claimed, that it was well beyond the capabilities of the independent photofinishers.

Since then there have been many improvements and modern colour films have many more than three colour-sensitive layers, but the principle has not changed.

1 http://www.rleggat.com/photohistory/index.html

2 http://www.photo.net/history/timeline

3 The Daguerreian Process: GEO. M. HOPKINS, Scientific American Vol. 56, No. 4, (22 January 1887) pp. 47, 52. See also www.daguerre.org

4 R.A.Hercock and G.A.Jones Silver by the Ton Mc Graw-Hill 1979 Page 14

5 R.A.Hercock and G.A.Jones Silver by the Ton Mc Graw-Hill 1979 Page 17

6 Rudolf Kingslake 1974 "The RochesteCamera and Lens Companies" Rochester NY, Photographic Historical Society and History of Kodak:George Eastman www.kodak.com

7 History of Kodak, www.kodak.com

8 R.A.Hercock and G.A.Jones Silver by the Ton Mc Graw-Hill 1979 page 28,29

9 Ferrania A Salmoiraghi

10 Frontiersman to Filmaker Birt Acre by A.B.Acres

11 R.A.Hercock and G.A.Jones Silver by the Ton Mc Graw-Hill 1979 Page 44

12 See United States v. Eastman Kodak Co., 226 F. 62, 79-80 (W.D.N.Y. 1915)

13 Coote Jack H. Photofinishing Techniques Focal Press 1970 P13

14 History of Kodak Cameras, Customer Service Pamphlet March 1999 . AA-13

15 Coote Jack H. Photofinishing Techniques Focal Press 1970 P47-53

CHAPTER 2

The Growth of Photography after World War 2

Innovation and very active promotion has resulted in a massive growth of photography during the last half-century.

World War 2 had taken its toll of many hobbies, and photography was no exception. Cameras and films were in short supply and in much of Europe and Japan the industry was in ruins. There was, however, a strong desire to get back to normality and the industry made a rapid recovery so that by 1947 photography was once again a popular hobby.

Most films were black and white and a far cry from those that we now take for granted. Many prints were still contact printed and enlargements were not very good, unless the film had been exposed in an expensive camera.

Contact printing meant using the largest possible negative, so 120 and 620 films, which can produce negatives and contact prints up to 6 x 9 cm (2 ¼" x 3 ¼"), were very common. For reasons of economy, the smaller 127 film had also become popular, especially when improvements in films and cameras allowed negatives to be enlarged.

In the US and the UK, 127 and 120 were the most popular sizes, with 35 mm used by the more advanced amateurs. On the other hand, in Japan and Germany, where there were a larger proportion of quality-conscious photographers, the proportion of 35 mm films was much higher. In France and Italy the proportion of roll films to 35 mm films was more evenly balanced.

From the 1960s onwards, 127 films and cameras were in decline, having been replaced by the 126 Instamatic format and today 120 roll films are mainly used by professional photographers.

In the 1940s Kodak were still by far the largest manufacturers of cameras, mainly ones which used 127 film, with smaller numbers for the 120 and 35 mm films. Many of the other manufacturers, especially in Europe, had been disrupted by the war and then restarted with models, which had not changed much from those that they had been producing in the thirties. With virtually no civilian production during the war years, there was an enormous pent-up demand for all types of photographic equipment.

Japan

By the late 1940s, several Japanese companies had started manufacturing cameras. At first they were sold only in Japan, but by 1950 they were being exported in small numbers to Europe and the US. To begin with, they were not very popular, because of strong anti-Japanese feelings, compounded by the awkward sounding names of the manufacturers.

Joe Ehrenreich, the New York based importer of Nippon Kogaku cameras, spent several years persuading the Japanese manufacturer that they needed a new name. When he finally succeeded, the Contax-like cameras appearing under the name Nikon, quickly became popular with the American public. [1] Similarly, the Precision Optical Industry Company, whose cameras resembled the Leica, was renamed Canon. By the late 1950s, many enthusiasts had discovered that Japanese cameras were equal to the best European and US models and cost considerably less. Gradually the anti-Japanese sentiment disappeared and their cameras became acceptable. The Japanese industry concentrated on 35mm cameras, which became very important later on.

Japan had many enthusiastic photographers who quickly turned to colour films when they became available in the fifties. The high cost of film, compared to incomes, was a problem, so several Japanese manufacturers introduced half-frame cameras, which could take 72 pictures on a standard length 35mm film. This format, however, did not catch on in Europe and the US, probably because cost-saving measures were not so important. For similar reasons, "wallet" sized prints, 2 ¼"x 3 ½" (6 x 9 cm) were much more popular in Japan than elsewhere.

During the fifties the majority of films were still black and white, but gradually colour transparencies, followed by colour prints, appeared. [2] Kodachrome transparencies, which had been introduced in the US in 1936, did not reach Europe in serious quantities until after the war. The availability of good-value Japanese 35 mm cameras undoubtedly helped to popularize them.

[3] Prior to World War 2, Agfacolor film had been produced in Wolfen in the Eastern part of the country and the paper in Leverkusen in the West. After the partition of Germany, it took Agfa some time to start film production in Leverkusen and it was not until 1949 that they were able to re-launch on the European market. Initially they produced colour negative film and colour paper, followed by Agfachrome transparency film in 1952.

[4] Kodak had introduced colour negative films and colour paper in the US in 1942, but it was many years before colour prints from negatives became popular. There were two main reasons for this. The quality of Kodachrome transparencies was far

superior to prints and colour prints were relatively expensive. The same situation applied later on for prints produced from Agfa-type materials.

There was, however, a considerable latent demand for colour prints provided they were of sufficient quality and affordable. In the US, both Kodak and Ansco produced a print material on a white plastic base for printing from transparencies. For some years, until prints from negatives were improved, they, and in particular Ansco Printon, were popular in the US; but more of that later.

By the late 1950s, prints from colour negatives had improved, although the results were variable. At their best, when the film had been correctly exposed and processed, they were very acceptable. Unfortunately, this was frequently not the case and many photographers stayed with black and white prints or colour transparencies.

The dyes in early colour negatives were not ideal and, in order to obtain bright prints, the film had to have a high contrast, which could result in degraded highlights and shadows. Another reason for inferior prints was that some of the dyes and colour couplers, which sensitized the films to the correct colours, were not very stable. All the manufacturers, but particularly Kodak, worked hard to improve this. The major step forward was to add a contrast-correction mask to the negative. This is the familiar orange mask. An interesting coincidence was that Eastman Kodak and GAF, whose film was called Plenacolor, filed patents for this on the same day. The addition of these masks dramatically improved colour negative films and further improvements have been made ever since. GAF found it difficult to compete with Kodak and a few years later abandoned amateur photography.

Early Kodacolor films were fairly grainy so that 35mm films were not introduced until 1958, many years after the roll-film formats. In 1963 Kodacolor X, a much-improved film, was introduced to coincide with the introduction of the Instamatic system – see later for more details. Further improvements followed in 1972 when a much finer grain version, called Kodakolor 2, was introduced and this resulted in a change of the process from C22 to C41, which is still used today

Kodak and Agfa Colour Negative Systems

By the late 1950s, there were two separate negative-positive systems, best described as the "Kodak" and "Agfa" systems. They differed in the way that they had solved some of the fundamentals of making colour films and papers; primarily the interaction of the different colour layers.

Initially there was probably not much to choose between the two systems as both had many shortcomings and the prints were only acceptable when all the conditions, such as exposure, storage of the films and processing, were optimum. The two systems required different processes, which was an inconvenience for photofinishers, but that was accepted while the market was growing rapidly.

Kodak had an advantage in that their system enabled them to use more stable dyes. The dyes used in colour films and prints in the 50s and 60s tended to fade within a few years, but this was somewhat less in Kodak prints than their competitors. It is no longer a serious problem, since by the end of the century, it was thought that most films and prints will be stable for 70 – 100 years.

As the quality of the films improved, Kodak began to dominate the US and many other markets, with the exception of Japan, which was heavily protected against outsiders.

By the time Kodacolor 2 and the C41 process were launched in 1972, the advantages of Kodacolor, together with Kodak's market domination, had made it very difficult to market non-Kodak compatible films. Fuji and Konica, who were anxious to export to the western markets, took out licences from Kodak and produced C41 compatible colour negative films. After a considerable amount of soul- searching, Agfa followed suit.

To understand Agfa's problem, one must go back forty or more years to the time when both Kodak and Agfa were very proud and, to many outsiders, seemed somewhat arrogant companies.

Kodak was a superb company, employing thousands of outstanding people who had, for more than half a century, pushed back the frontiers of photographic technology and produced any number of very profitable products much loved by their customers. A by-product of this was that many within Kodak believed that the company could do no wrong; so much so, that they would never admit to a customer that they had supplied a faulty product. The comment was, "It just does not happen at Kodak", so the story goes. That attitude took some years of very bruising competition to change.

Agfa was similarly an excellent company, which in the mid-thirties was the first company to solve the problem of different colour film layers interacting with each other which allowed them to launch colour negative and cine films in 1936. This made it very hard for them to accept the idea of adopting the Kodak system for colour films. There were no doubt many reasons to be proud of their achievements. However, some of its more insular members took this rather too far, believing that they had invented photography and the world was at their feet. Not too many outsiders believed this and as over the years Kodak, followed by Fuji, took commanding leads in the industry, attitudes gradually changed.

Luckily there were many insiders who did not always take themselves, or Agfa, too seriously and there were many amusing stories circulating the corridors below top management. In the seventies there was the story, told by one of the marketing managers, about the "Herr Director" of the Munich camera works, who asked the newly arrived intern: "If the world were to end tomorrow, what would you do?" Without a moment's hesitation, the bright young man quipped, "I would take the first train to the head office in Leverkusen, where things always happen four years later".

The standardization of colour processes, not to mention improvements in quality, helped the growth of photography, especially amongst snap-shooters. Right from the time when George Eastman set out to simplify photography, the popularity of amateur photography had been linked to its ease of use. There were many developments in this period which greatly simplified photography and considerably improved the chances of producing good pictures.

Instamatic

For many people, particularly women, loading the film and taking it out of the camera was a frightening experience. There was the worry of whether the light was sufficiently subdued and there was always the chance that the backing paper would spring loose allowing light to leak onto the film. No doubt a significant number of films were spoilt and this acted as a discouragement to popular photography. Kodak took a big step forward when they introduced 126 Instamatic films and cameras in 1963. The film was supplied in a light-tight plastic cartridge which incorporated both the feed and take-up spools so that there was no need to thread the film into the camera. This simplified the process of loading the camera and greatly reduced the chance of a spoilt film. The Instamatic system replaced the low-cost box cameras, which had been responsible for much of the growth prior to this.

The Instamatic film was 35 mm wide, which fitted in well with the equipment used for processing. It differed from normal 35 mm film in that there was only one perforation per frame and a pre-exposed narrow border round the frame, which took care of any errors in the film advance of the cameras. While Instamatics made an ideal successor to the low-cost box cameras, they had two limitations. The picture produced was square, which was not to everyone's taste and in 1963 the plastic cartridge would not allow the film to lie as flat in the camera as it would in a good quality, metal-body 35 mm camera. This restricted the sharpness of the image and hence the size to which it could be enlarged. To be fair to Kodak, the market for which it was intended did not include many large prints.

The Instamatic system was a great success and in the following seven years Kodak manufactured more than[5] 50 million cameras. The system was licensed to other manufacturers who produced both films and cameras.

126 and 110 Instamatic Films

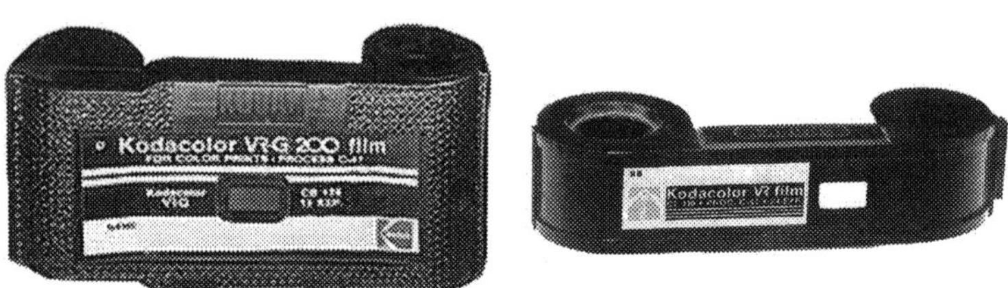

In 1972, when they introduced the improved Kodacolor 2 film, Kodak extended the system by introducing 110 film, a miniature version, using 16 mm wide film and producing rectangular pictures. It became very popular and Kodak produced more than 25 million pocket Instamatic cameras, as they were called, over the next three years. [6] The cameras were small and easy to carry and this no doubt contributed to their popularity.

The Instamatic system, particularly the 110, demonstrated the great improvements in film quality and low-cost lenses in that prints, mostly 3 ½" (89mm) wide could now be produced from much smaller negatives than previously. It almost certainly helped Kodak to become one of the World's most profitable companies. Charging a higher price per film, at the same time as reducing the amount of film in each cartridge, must be the marketing managers' dream, but few, other than Kodak in the 1970s, achieved it.

Automatic Exposure Control

Another development, which helped photography grow, was automatic exposure control. This had first been incorporated in a Kodak camera in 1938, [7] but to be realistic, did not catch on until much later. Some of the upmarket cameras incorporated an exposure meter, but this had to be set manually, usually by turning a dial until a pointer was lined up with a mark. Fully automatic exposure control in low- cost cameras did not catch on until the 1970s. When it finally became common in even fairly low-cost cameras, it increased the number of correctly exposed negatives and therefore the number of acceptable prints. This certainly helped to popularize photography and fuel its growth.

As well as automatic exposure control, there was another development, which was probably even more important. Early colour films had very little exposure latitude. If the exposure had been incorrect, it was difficult to produce good prints. The maximum exposure error in order to produce acceptable prints was +/- 1 stops. A stop is the calibration on the lens diaphragm, each stop halving or doubling the amount of light which falls on the film. There has been continuous development to increase the latitude and the latest colour negative films will give very acceptable prints even if they are three stops over or under-exposed.

There is, of course, more to making good pictures than just exposure control. One can summarize the elements of making good pictures as follows.

- Compose the picture – this depends on the photographer's judgement.
- Set the correct exposure.
- Produce a sharp image.
- Hold the camera still while taking the picture.

By the seventies, correct exposure had been largely taken care of by a combination of increased exposure latitude of the films and automatic exposure control.

Obtaining a sharp image was a bit more difficult. Simple cameras usually have small aperture lenses and this gives them a good depth of focus. However, the small aperture means that they work best in bright sunshine. In low light conditions the exposures would be rather long, which makes holding the camera still rather difficult. A way round this was to fit a larger aperture lens which could be focused, but this meant either judging the distance or in the case of the more expensive cameras, fitting a range-finder.

Disc

In the late seventies, Kodak devised a revolutionary system to produce "Decision Free" photography. After about five years of work by several thousand people in complete secrecy, they took the industry by complete surprise in early [8] 1982 by announcing their Disc films and cameras.

The idea was to produce a camera, small enough to fit into a shirt pocket, which could be pointed at a subject and, without adjusting the exposure or focus, would produce a good picture.

The starting point was a colour negative film, type VR100, with new T-grain emulsion technology, which had a much higher resolution than previous films. Due to this high resolution, even a very small negative would produce an acceptable print.

The knock-on effect of the small negative format was that the cameras could have large- aperture, short-focal-length lenses, which would produce sharp images from quite close up right up to infinity. An additional bonus, with the small negatives and short focal length lenses was that the cameras were very compact.

Fifteen frames of film, each 8 x 11 mm, were mounted like petals, on the periphery of a plastic disc. The disc was placed inside a light-tight cassette, similar to, but considerably smaller than, a floppy computer disc. Loading and unloading the camera was very simple.

Disc Camera, Processed Film and Film Cassette

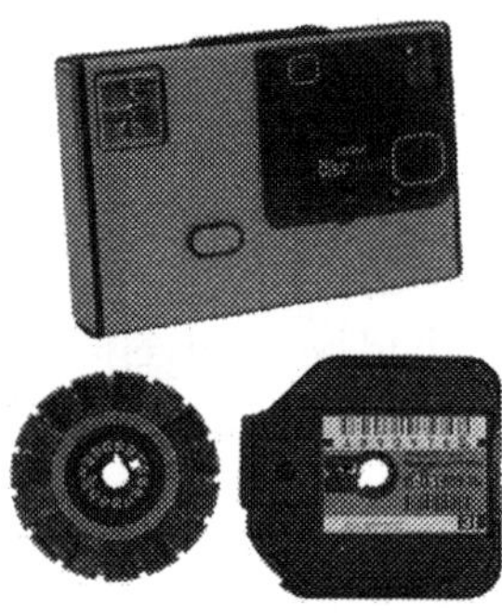

There were a number of other potential, although never realized, features of the system. One was the fact that the cassettes could have been handled completely automatically at the processing stage, opening up the possibility of self-service developing and printing, which by the Millenium still did not exist.

Kodak's launch of the system was very impressive and at the time convinced many, including the author, that this was a major advance. At the launch, Kodak produced not only the films and cameras, but complete sets of very revolutionary equipment for developing the films and producing the prints. Furthermore, Kodak offered licences, for their numerous equipment patents, to the rest of the industry so that they could produce cameras and photofinishing equipment.

Another unusual feature of the launch was how Kodak had managed to keep the work of several thousand people secret for five or more years. It speaks very highly of how Kodak was regarded by the people of Rochester. This is probably unique in peacetime industrial history.

The disc system was not the success that it might have been. There had been extensive tests of the system by Kodak staff but, unfortunately, these did not show up some of the flaws, or possibly if they did, they were either ignored or not considered to be serious. The most serious problem was that production batches of the film were not up to the standard of the experimental films. As a result, many of the prints were either not sharp or were very grainy. In addition, the test cameras were probably rather better than some of the cheaper production cameras.

To make matters worse, several Japanese companies shortly afterwards introduced autofocus, easy load, compact 35mm cameras. These had all the advantages of decision-free photography, but with a much superior quality. Against these, the highly attractive small size of the disc cameras was not enough to sell the system in sufficient numbers.

Kodak persevered for a few years but stopped production of the cameras in 1987.

An interesting speculation is that, had the 1982 films been up to the quality of today's films, would the disc system have been a success? Nobody will ever know the answer to this question.

The compact, fully automatic, auto-focus cameras of the nineteen eighties and much improved colour negative films, gave popular photography another boost.

In the early nineties, a consortium of major film and camera manufacturers set about developing a new film format and the corresponding cameras. There were a number of stated aims, which included making it easier for the amateur photographer to produce good pictures and reducing the size of the cameras.

APS – The Advanced Photo System

In early 1996, Kodak, Fuji, Canon, Nikon and Olympus launched the Advanced Photo System (APS), using a 24mm wide film in a cassette. The film, in addition to its emulsion, had a transparent magnetic coating on the back. The consortium of five companies, which were later joined by others, laid down various standards, but left a number of options for the different manufacturers to take up. The principal features included three formats: the Classic, the High-Definition TV and the Panorama format, which can all be selected on the camera and are automatically produced when the negatives are printed. The magnetic coating is used to record data for this and other features, some of which are unique to individual manufacturers.

Another important aim of APS was to eliminate the nearly 3% of 35 mm films, sent to photofinishers, which were faulty, due to incorrect loading or unloading of the cameras. This is very unlikely to happen with an APS camera. At the same time, many manufacturers introduced easy-load 35mm cameras, so that by the Millenium this may not have been quite so important.

The Advanced Photo System was jointly developed by some of the leading companies in the industry and this made the launch easier than the disc system launch had been. However, the fact that the films could not be processed by photofinishers until they had put in substantial additional equipment, slowed its growth and it took several years until the APS volume had reached 10% of colour films. Some in the industry questioned whether many of its features could not have been added to 35mm films.

Single-use Cameras

The fastest growing segment of photography at the Millenium was the single, or one-time use camera. They were Introduced by Fuji in 1986, followed soon afterwards by Kodak and Agfa. Initially they were called "disposable" cameras, but this was found to be an unsuitable name. One-time use is not strictly correct as, after processing, the components are retrieved from photofinishers and used to build further cameras. Some of the components are reused five or six times. In Japan they are called a "film with lens" to emphasize the recycling aspect.

Instant Photography

Instant photography, which produced a finished print a short time after the picture was taken, was invented by Edwin Herbert Land, the founder of the Polaroid Corporation. Land's achievement was to incorporate the processing chemicals into the film. The processing chemicals were contained in tiny capsules, which were squeezed to apply the chemicals to the film when the film was wound on after making the exposure. The first black and white Polaroid cameras and films were marketed in November 1948. Due to their novelty, they were a great success, especially in the United States. [9] In 1963 a colour process called Polacolor was introduced and soon Polaroid became the second largest photographic company in the world.

Both the black and white and the Polacolor processes relied on a receiving sheet for the final image and this resulted in a rather messy peel-off part, which had to be discarded. In 1972, Polaroid introduced the SX 70, a very much improved camera and process, which ejected the finished colour print from the camera without the need to peel off this part. It was a remarkable development and, furthermore, to solve another problem of simple picture taking, it was the first time that a popular camera incorporated an autofocus lens. The camera and film were an immediate success and became very popular, particularly in the US.

In Europe and Japan, Polaroid cameras were considered more of a fun device than for serious photography and the numbers sold were considerably fewer than in the US. Polaroid films were, and still are, also used for a number of professional purposes all over the world.

Because of the considerable success of Polaroid, Kodak felt it had to develop its own instant films and launched its own version in April 1975, claiming that it did not infringe Polaroid's many patents. Six days later, Polaroid launched a legal action against Kodak, which they eventually won. Ten years later, Kodak withdrew all their cameras and film.

In 1990 Kodak paid Polaroid about $900 million damages, including interest. This was in addition to the astronomical cost of recalling cameras and film and compensating users, not to mention the enormous investment in R&D, production facilities and world-wide distribution. Rumour had it that, for the first time in history, Kodak borrowed money from the banks after this! Whether that was true or not, it was a serious financial set back.

Fuji took out a licence from Polaroid and introduced its own version of instant films, which were still available in 2004.

By the end of the century, instant photography accounted for about 10% of the total of amateur photography, yet its long-term future must be somewhat questionable now that the number of digital cameras is increasing rapidly. Polaroid cameras have always suffered from being either very large or producing small prints. Digital cameras are generally much smaller and, although they cannot produce instant prints, usually incorporate a screen where one can see the results immediately, which usually suffices for most people.

It is sad that, in 2002, Polaroid filed for bankruptcy protection and to a large extent survives by licensing out its brand name to other manufacturers.

During the period of the second half of the 20th century there has been remarkable growth and development in photography. At the beginning of the period the vast majority of photographs were black and white. These were gradually joined by color transparencies, followed by color prints and now, at the beginning of the 21st century, digital photography is growing rapidly.

In most countries, with the exception of China, India and some other developing markets, where photography is growing rapidly, sales of colour films started declining in 2001, except for SUC (Single Use Camera) cameras whose sales are still increasing year by year, albeit slowly. The wheel seems to have turned a full circle in the last 100 years since George Eastman introduced cameras which were sent back to Kodak to have the film developed and then returned to the customer refilled with a fresh film. The only difference is that the recycled SUC camera, loaded with fresh film, is sent back to the shop for resale.

A good example of the growth of photography is what has happened in the UK. Between 1960 and 2000, amateur photography has grown by a factor of about 30. In countries with more sunshine, like the United States, the growth has been even greater.

Black and white and transparencies now each comprise less than 10% of the total in most markets, although the proportions vary from country to country. Some people had pronounced black and white dead, but this is far from true, in fact In many markets there has been a revival. It is anyone's guess what the next 50 years will bring.

So what is the situation now compared with that at the end of World War 2? In 1946, with the exception of the United States and to a lesser extent the UK, amateur photography was – on a very small scale – enjoyed by only a small proportion of the population. There were a small number of manufacturers producing films and papers, most of whom, with the exception of Kodak, only operated in their home country.

Now, early in the 21st century, most families in the developed world, with the possible exception of the very poorest, have a camera and take pictures to record their life. As a result, we have an industry whose numbers are beyond the comprehension of ordinary mortals. In 2002, worldwide, some 100 billion images were exposed on film, most of which were printed in colour. In addition, some 78 billion images were captured digitally of which possibly one-third were printed[10]. In the US alone each year there are more than 25 billion pictures taken, mostly made into colour prints.

There have been considerable changes among the manufacturers of film and paper, most of whom now operate globally. The dominant names are Kodak and Fuji and the considerably smaller Agfa, Ferrania, Konica and Mitsubishi. There are some other manufacturers, but these are not generally involved in the amateur market except in China and India. From 2003 onwards there has been a rapid decline in sales of film cameras and consequently colour film and, to a lesser extent, paper.

Late in 2005 Agfa ceased to trade and early in 2006, Konica, who had previously merged their business with Minolta, announced that they would exit the photographic industry and cease producing film and paper by early 2007. Judging by the decline of film sales in recent years, it seems as if they could become a niche product within a few years.

A very major change has been the growth of digital photography or digital imaging as it is now called. Kodak and Fuji, even if only to defend their market position, are very active in this area, as are most of the traditional camera manufacturers. However, a number of electronics companies led by Sony, Hewlett Packard and Epson (Seiko) are staking out their place and offering complete systems from camera to print or screen. The whole industry, including photofinishing is, as we will see, changing rapidly.

1 Canon Website
2 Kodak Website Milestones 1933–1979
3 [1] The Illustrated History of Colour Photography, Jack H Coote CH 9
4 Kodak Website Milestones 1933–1979
5 Kodak Website Milestones 1963
6 Kodak Website Milestones 1972
7 Kodak Website Milestones 1938
8 Kodak Website Milestones 1982
9 The Illustrated History of Colour Photography, Jack H Coote CH 14, P221
10 IDC forecast 2002

CHAPTER 3

The Photofinishing Industry and its Technology

What is the Photofinishing Industry ?

There are hundreds of thousands of people working world-wide to develop and print our films. The vast majority will be working for amateurs, holiday snap photographers, and those for whom photography is simply a hobby. However some, using the same or very similar technology, will be working for social photographers who might be taking pictures of school children, weddings or other similar events.

During the first half of the twentieth century, almost all films were used to produce black and white (B &W) prints. Colour transparencies, or slide films, were introduced in the late 1930s, but with the advent of World War 2, did not become widespread until the 1950s. It was shortly after this, that colour negatives and colour print films appeared on the scene. Now, at the start of the 21st century, we have all three types of film, as well as prints and images, which are produced without any film at all.

Black and white prints are made from a negative film. The image formed inside the camera on this type of film is reversed after development, with the brightest part forming the darkest image on the film. This is neither very convenient, nor easy to view. If we now project the image which is on the negative film onto a piece of photographic paper, a further reversal takes place and after processing we will have a picture which is a very close replica of that originally captured by the camera.

The way this happens is that, when we expose a black and white film to light, some of the silver halide, the light sensitive component of the emulsion, is converted into a latent image. This latent image is not visible to the naked eye. However, if we place the film in a developer solution, a chemical reaction takes place in which the latent image is converted into metallic silver, which blocks out the light and therefore appears black. In the case of a negative film, if we now place the film into a fixing solution, such as sodium thiosulphate, commonly known as “hypo”, the remaining silver halide dissolves, leaving a reversed black silver image.

An alternative is, after the developer stage, to place the film into a bleaching solution. This removes the metallic silver, but leaves the remaining unexposed silver halide unaffected. If we now expose the film to light, the remaining unexposed silver halide forms another latent image, and, after further development and fixing, an image similar to that originally “seen” by the camera will result. This is the basic method for producing a black & white transparency or slide.

When colour pictures are taken, the film produces a negative, which consists of superimposed, yellow, magenta and cyan coloured reversed images. Similarly colour paper has three superimposed layers, producing yellow, magenta and cyan images.

Colour print production is similar to black and white except that, when the negative film is projected onto the colour paper, each of the three coloured layers of the film only affects one of the three layers of the paper, reversing the images to produce an image as originally "seen" by the camera. This is quite a complicated process, which has taken many years to perfect.

In the case of colour film, the silver halide in each of the layers, which are respectively sensitised to blue, green and red light, contains in addition, a colour coupler which, during development, forms a dye in amounts which are proportional to the silver image. After development the silver is removed by means of a bleaching solution leaving yellow, magenta and cyan dyes in the appropriate layers. The remaining unexposed silver halide is removed with a fixing solution.

The same options, as for black and white films, are also available for negatives and transparencies. If we produce a colour negative film, it is projected onto colour paper to produce the final image. This is normally known as printing.

The alternative is to reverse the image in the film, in order to produce a colour transparency. We do this by developing the image as exposed by the camera, but without generating the dyes. The film is then re-exposed to light* which forms latent images in the remaining silver halide and these are now developed, this time forming the yellow, magenta and cyan coloured layers. Finally, the remaining silver is removed by bleaching. This in principal is the way in which most colour transparencies, with the exception of Kodachrome, are produced.

The very first photofinishing operations were rather different to what happens today. The process was completely new and there was no suitable technology available. George Eastman, who successfully sold films and cameras at that time, had to invent a method for developing and printing the films that his customers were returning.

The principles of Developing & Printing (D&P), at least for black and white films, have hardly changed over the last hundred years. First the exposed film is placed in a solution of developer, it then spends some time in a solution of fix, after which it is washed, in order to remove the remains of the chemicals. Finally, the film is hung up to dry.

**Most reversal or transparency processes have now replaced the re-exposure with a chemical process.*

The next stage is to print the film onto photographic paper. In the early days, a frame was used, which clamped the film into contact with the paper. A light was then shone through the film. Kodak's first works in Rochester and Harrow used daylight to expose the prints by placing the frames near to a window. After exposing in this way, the paper was treated in a similar manner to the film, being placed successively in solutions of developer and fix, followed by washing and drying. Apart from exposing the prints, all the work had to be done under safe light conditions, that is, under yellow/orange light, to which the paper and film are very insensitive. This usually involved covering the windows with yellow paper.

Kodak D & P 1908

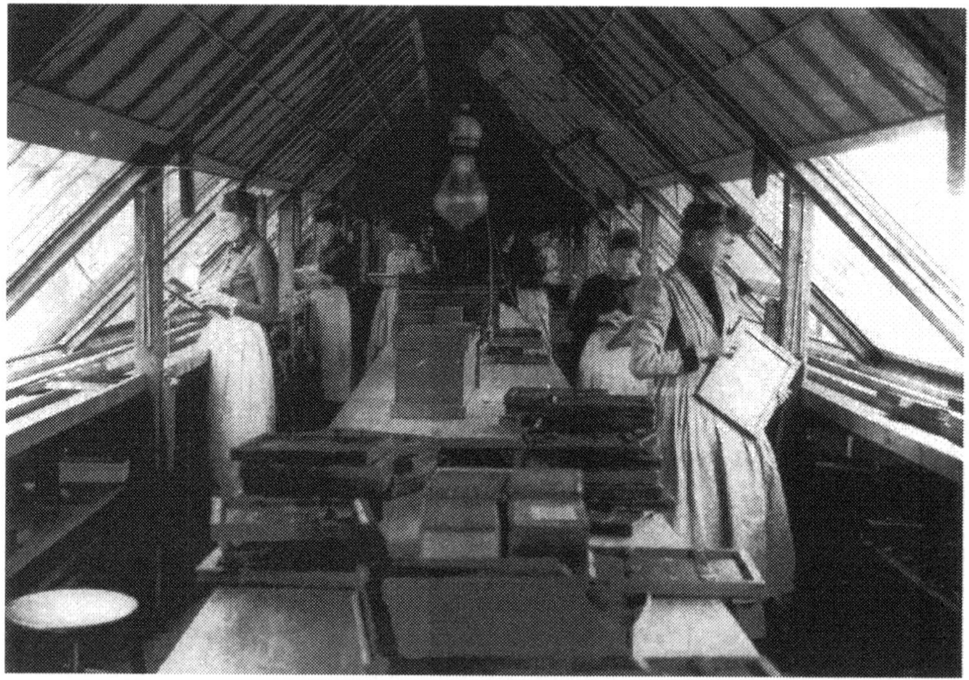

Equipment in the early years was fairly simple. The processing containers, in which the films were developed, fixed and washed, were vertical tanks, often made from a length of earthenware drainpipe with one end blocked. After processing the films were hung up to dry.

The paper was processed in shallow tanks, sometimes made of wood lined with roofing felt or bitumen. The only way of controlling the development of the prints was to watch them under safe light and then to move them from the developer to the fix when the image appeared to be correct.

These early pioneers soon discovered how difficult it was to obtain consistent results, as batches of films varied and the need to control the developers was not yet understood. During the printing stage, corrections had to be made to compensate for these variations.

Quite early on in the century, photographic view postcards became very popular and, as printing these involved making large numbers of prints from a single negative, some of the pioneers quickly developed an assortment of equipment in order to streamline the process. [1]

Photofinishing Emerges

At first, independent photofinishing grew quite slowly. Some of the studios, who took portraits, also sold cameras and films, and so they offered to do the amateur's developing and printing themselves to avoid having to send the films back to Kodak. In other cases, pharmacists, who were supplying chemicals to amateurs, also started to develop and print. As the number of films grew, a new type of business emerged, mainly in the US and the UK, developing and printing films for camera shops and chemists. This was the beginning of wholesale photofinishing.

The photofinishers needed to process the films speedily to achieve a quick turnaround. Many designed equipment for their own laboratories, but some started manufacturing machinery for use by others. One example was William Barker who had started the Roll Film Company in London soon after World War 1. Another was Cecil Hepworth, who was a UK photofinisher. Both men built semi-automatic film developing machines, some of which were still in operation after World War 2.

Barker also built other pieces of equipment, notably a machine for printing onto paper in rolls, as well as a roll-paper processing machine and an automatic cutter for cutting the strips of prints into individual prints. This was very advanced for the time, but there were major difficulties in avoiding "crossovers", that is the mixing up of different customers' orders. This is a problem which, even today, photofinishers have to grapple with, including the largest companies, who may handle up to 100,000 films on a busy day. However, the use of modern systems and equipment have mainly solved this problem.[2]

Pako

Glen Dye, in the US, was working on a much larger scale. He had been building processing equipment since 1909 and is best known as the founder of the Pako Corporation of Minneapolis which, by the 60s and 70s, had become the worlds largest manufacturer of printing and processing equipment, with a turnover of about $90m. Dye was one of the earliest US photofinishers and quickly set about designing automatic equipment, initially for his own laboratory and later on for general sale. Eventually, the Pako manufacturing business became far larger than its photofinishing lab.

Over the years, Dye produced a complete range of machines for processing films, and for exposing and processing prints. His early film processors were of the "dip and dunk" type and similar machines have since been manufactured by many other companies.

Dip and dunk processors, with the exception of the dryer, are normally placed in a darkroom. The operator unrolls the films and clips them to a hanger bar, which he places on two hooks close to the first processing tank and then clips a weight to the other end of each film to make them hang vertically side by side. Depending on the size of the machine, each hanger takes three to eight films.

Dip and Dunk Film Processor

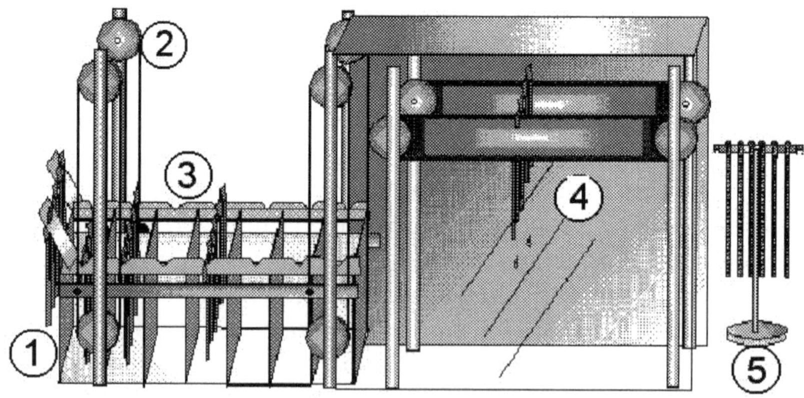

1 Loading rack
2 Lifting mechanism
3 Chemical and wash tanks
4 Drying cabinet with film conveyor
5 Stand (or rack) for processed films

The tanks containing the processing solutions and wash water are placed in a row and a mechanism, situated above the tanks, picks up the hanger bars, and lifts them so that the bottom of the films are above the top of the tanks, transports them forward until they are over the first tank and then lowers them. Once in the tank, another mechanism moves the bars forward until the films are ready to be lifted out and placed into the next tank. This procedure continues for each stage of the process in the sequence of develop, fix and wash. The time interval between each lift is adjusted so that the films are immersed in the solutions for the correct amount of time. After the last tank a light trap allows the bars and films to be passed into a heated drying cabinet through which they are transported by a conveyor.

Glyn Dye's company, Pako, not only produced film processors, but also a huge range of other machines including both contact and projection printers, paper processors and cutters to chop up the prints into individual photos. As time progressed, other companies also produced photofinishing equipment. Among these were: Kodak, both in Rochester and England; Ilford and Williamson in England; and Agfa in Germany.

By the beginning of World War 2, although some photofinishers were printing onto roll paper, the majority were still using sheet paper. There were a number of reasons for this, not least being the unwillingness of photofinishers to invest in complicated equipment. Many of the workers were very dextrous in handling the sheets of paper and, considering the level of wages in the 30s, the advantages of mechanisation were somewhat marginal. However, there was another reason, which was particularly relevant in quality conscious countries like Germany. To obtain optimum quality, it was necessary to use several types of paper, each with a different contrast, depending on the subject and exposure of the negative and this meant printing onto individual sheets. The problem continued until many years later, when variable contrast papers became available.

During the thirties, due to the improvements in film quality, which had increased the popularity of the smaller 127 and 35 mm negatives, there was a movement from contact to enlarged prints. In some countries, such as France, Germany and Italy, this was carried out using enlargers built by, amongst others, Leitz and Agfa. In the US and the UK, where roll paper had become popular, printers, known as "roll head printers", came into use. These were generally devices of fixed magnification, which were set up to make one print size. It was possible to cater for different film sizes by changing the lens and negative carrier. In the earliest printers, exposure was controlled by the operators, who used their own judgement to adjust either the time or lamp intensity. Gradually the machines became more sophisticated and, from the early 30s, some of the printers were fitted with photocells to measure, and eventually to control, the exposures.

The developing and printing of colour, especially colour negative films, is considerably more complicated than the processing of black and white films and prints.

The chemical processes require very strict controls with regard to time, temperature and the state of the chemistry. In the early days, this would almost certainly have involved frequent analysis to determine the quantity of the solutions that had been used up and how much fresh chemistry needed to be added to replenish them.

Colour processing must be carried out in complete darkness and it is therefore not possible to assess the prints visually in the developer.

At the printing stage, both the exposure and colour must be assessed and controlled in order to make a correct print.

Kodak went to great lengths to reduce these variations, but it was not easy and consequently took many years. By 1942, when colour prints became available, black and white films were being processed in automatic dip and dunk processors and prints were being produced on rolls and processed in continuous paper processors. These machines now had to be adapted for colour.

The processing of colour films and prints requires more chemical stages than does black and white, so the colour processing machines need to have more tanks. To obtain consistent results, it was important to provide accurate temperature control and also to replenish the solutions by adding fresh chemicals in quantities which were proportional to the area of film or paper processed. The solution tanks were fitted with circulation pumps, heaters, thermostats and metering devices to add the fresh chemistry.

The biggest change arose in the equipment needed for exposing the colour prints. Black and white printers at that time had photocells, which measured the light falling onto the printing paper, and these were used to control either the length of exposure or the brightness of the printing lamp. Making a colour print is equivalent to making three superimposed prints, coloured respectively yellow, magenta and cyan, and the exposures for each of these have to be individually controlled.

The simplest way of doing this is to expose the three coloured images separately by exposing each in turn through blue, green and red filters*. Each of the three exposures can be adjusted by trial and error or can be controlled by a photocell

**Blue, green and red are complementary colours to yellow magenta and cyan. The intensity of the blue light falling on the paper, will only be affected by the yellow layer of the film, similarly the green light by the magenta layer and the red light by the cyan layer.*

in much the same way as had previously been done for black and white printing. However, this is not quite as simple as it sounds and has occupied the minds of many very clever people for the past 60 years.

Colour Printing – Integration to Grey

The most fundamental criterion was first described in 1938 by Pitt and Selwyn, from Kodak's UK Research Labs.[3] It is known as "integration to grey", and is based on the discovery that the average colour of most outdoor subjects is grey. This can easily be put to the test by placing a number of snapshots on a turn-table, which is spinning sufficiently fast to blur the pictures. All the pictures appear to be grey or slightly tinted grey. It was this discovery which resulted in the methods used to control the exposures of the three-colour paper images.

This means that, in order to obtain a correctly exposed picture, it is necessary to control the intensity of each of the three exposures, so that when viewing the prints, if the light from them were to be scrambled, they would appear to be grey. In its simplest form this involves adjusting the three exposures so that the light falling on the paper is in a certain ratio and intensity, irrespective of the densities of the three layers of the negative. However, in practice, things are rather more complicated.

Once Kodacolor was released in 1942, Kodak set up a processing lab in Rochester to serve the US market. The film and paper processing equipment were based on the same machines as had been used for black and white, but somewhat extended and refined in order to cope with the complexity of the colour processes.

The existing black and white printers were not originally considered to be suitable for adaptation to colour, although that did, in fact, happen later and Eastman Kodak designed a very elaborate machine to do it. The Eastman Kodak type 1599 printers exposed each negative in turn through blue, green and red filters. The three exposures were set to be of equal time, about ½ second, but before making the exposures, the intensity of the printing light was measured by photocells and adjusted so that the amount of light which reached the paper would produce the "integrated to grey" image.

The system of "integration to grey" is far from perfect as there are a significant number of scenes which do not conform to this rule, so the printers had to be provided with over-ride controls in order that manual corrections could be made. In some cases a skilled operator was able to detect which negatives would not provide an optimum print under automatic control and could thus make corrections before printing. However, this was more commonly done when remaking unsatisfactory prints.

The Eastman-type 1559 printers were, in the main, used with 120-sized negatives cut into single frames. To speed up the operation, three prints were produced side by side on a wide roll of paper and then separated after processing. The printer had three negative carriers so that the operator was able to change a negative in one of them, while the printer was making an exposure from another. This would allow a skilled operator to produce 1000 prints per hour. These printers were in use in Rochester for over twenty years, but were considered to be too complicated for sale to independent photofinishers.

Over the next 20 years Kodak were by far the most successful company in the photographic industry, and thus were frequently the target of numerous much smaller companies, which attempted to obtain a slice of the giant's business.

Colortron printers are an interesting example how in the late 1950s it was possible for one or two talented people, working for a small company, to produce a product in many ways in advance of those produced by much larger companies such as Eastman Kodak or Pako.

"Additive" Printing

Eastman Kodak, in order to comply with the US consent decree in 1954 had to provide independent photofinishers with a colour printer and they did this by adapting a B&W model to produce their model 4C colour printer. This involved fitting 3 colour filters, blue, green and red, to come into the light path in sequence and using three photocells, looking at the negative, to control the three exposures. The printers had to be operated in semi-darkness, as any ambient light would also affect the photocells and hence the exposures. A further complication was that the printers had to make at least two sizes of prints and accept several negative sizes. Each combination of negative and print size, not to mention paper batch or negative type, required a different setting for the photocells. The printers were fitted with a large number of potentiometers, grouped in banks of three, one for each colour, which all had to be adjusted by making test prints, a fairly skilled and tedious procedure. To add to the complications, various other settings had to be made by trial and error to set slope compensation to take care of the non-linearity of the films and papers.

Additive Printer

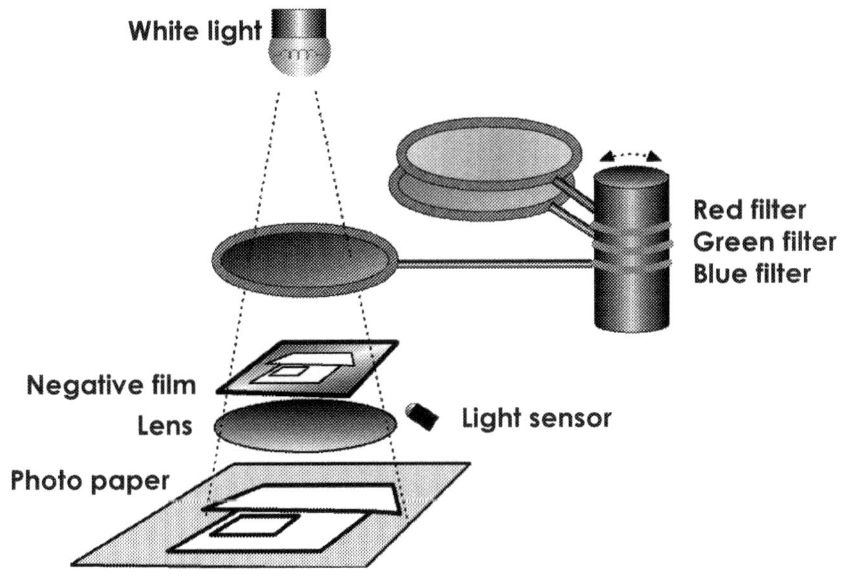

By contrast Keith Aston and his colleague Geoffrey Long, the designers of the Colortron printers, produced an altogether much simpler and pleasanter to operate device. As in the case of the Eastman Kodak model 4C, it made three successive exposures through blue, green and red filters but, being completely light tight, it could operate in bright ambient light without affecting the light sensor. The exposures were controlled by a photomultiplier cell measuring the light reflected from the paper which meant that only a very simple compensation for print size, set at the time of manufacture, was required and this removed the need to adjust large numbers of channels for different negative sizes. They also devised an extremely simple way to set up slope compensation, which improves the results from over and underexposed negatives. In its time it was the most stable and easy to set up colour printer available and this helped in the production of a high proportion of good prints.

These features made the printers particularly suitable for smaller photofinishers who did not have an army of highly trained technicians. Not surprisingly, the company, employing less than 10 people, found it difficult to market the printers in competition with Kodak, Agfa and Pako and as a result had only limited success in Europe. However it was very successful in Japan, where Fuji recognising its features, used it to establish their market leadership in colour print films – see chapter on Japanese labs.

To put it into perspective, the Colortron additive printers were slower than the Kodak, Pako or Agfa printers and by the mid 1960s were no longer used for amateur photofinishing other than in Japan. However, a few years later the company became very successful worldwide with their Miniprinter, an even simpler device and a range of printers for use by social photographers and custom labs.

Agfa's first colour printers were also additive but they speeded them up by fitting the lamp house with three lamps and making the blue, green and red exposures simultaneously. However, as competition required ever faster printers and with improvements in filter technology, they, as most other manufacturers, changed to subtractive printing, see later.

By the end of the fifties a large number of US photofinishers were processing Kodacolor film, while several other film manufacturers had themselves started producing colour negative film. The main players were Agfa in Germany, Ferrania in Italy, Gevaert in Belgium, Ilford in the UK, and Fuji, Konishiroku and Oriental in Japan. There were also a few other, much smaller, companies such as Pakolor in the UK.

This spurred on a thriving equipment industry, in particular Pako in the US, who produced a complete range of equipment, which included colour printers. Other companies who also produced such printers were Agfa and Müllersohn in Germany, Priox in France, Kodak and Colortron, an offshoot of Packolor, in the UK, and (some years later) Gretag in Switzerland. Fuji and Sakura (later called Konica) manufactured colour printers and Noritsu processing machines in Japan. Still later, several Italian companies, including San Marco, Safai, AFI and Italfoto also produced colour printing and processing equipment. Other companies involved in manufacturing processing equipment included Refrema in Denmark, Hostert in Germany and Wainco in the UK.

The development of these colour printers is very interesting. At first glance it might appear to be a simple matter. If the colour films were able to sense the subject correctly, all that would be necessary in order to produce a correct print, would be to shine a suitably coloured light through the negative. However, this ignores the fact that the light, under which amateur photographs are taken, varies from picture to picture. When we look at a scene, our eyes automatically compensate for the different lighting, but the film does not and so we need to find ways of producing a realistic-looking picture when we are producing the prints. This was the reason why, for many years, it was necessary to adopt the "integration to grey" approach to exposure and colour measurement.

Professional photographers, who take all their pictures in a studio under fixed lighting conditions, do not have this problem and so it is much simpler for them to select the correct exposure for their prints.

"Subtractive" Printers

Kodak's UK research laboratories employed some very talented people who designed colour printers using a different system, which was subsequently adopted by most other manufacturers, including the parent company, Eastman Kodak. Instead of making three exposures in turn through blue, green and red filters, called additive printing, they made one exposure with white light, which includes the blue, green and red light to which the yellow, magenta and cyan coloured layers are sensitive. When sufficient of the blue light has passed, a yellow filter, which cuts off the blue light, is placed into the light path. This allows the green and red light to continue exposing the magenta and cyan coloured layers. In turn magenta and cyan coloured filters, which cut off the green and red light, are brought into the light path thereby terminating the exposure. From a light point of view, this is much more efficient, greatly reducing the exposure times and thus speeding up the printers. In theory there should not be any difference in the quality obtained by the two methods. However, in the earlier days, due to shortcomings in the filters, as well as limitations caused by certain characteristics of the films and colour papers, the prints produced on additive printers were of a slightly better quality than those produced by this method.

Subtractive Printers

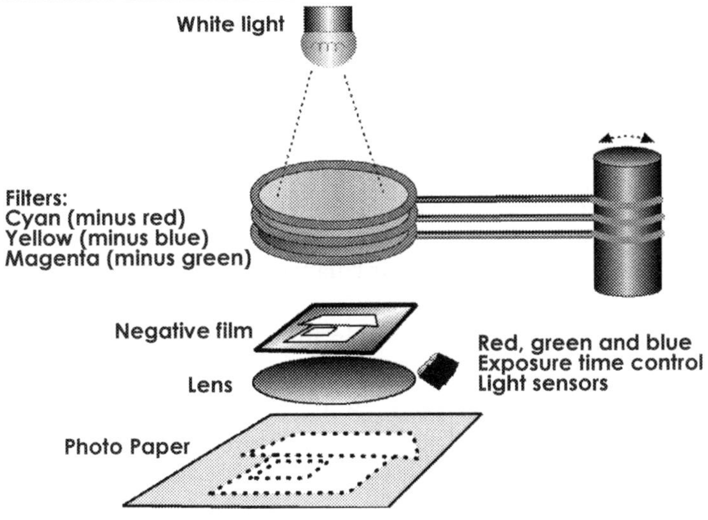

These printers were known as "subtractive" printers, and their introduction began a period of more than 30 years, during which the various manufacturers worked to improve the speed, but possibly more importantly the quality, of prints produced. By the end of the 1950s, colour printers could produce 300 – 1000 prints per hour, but with a significant quantity of rejects, which then had to be reprinted. The number of reprints varied considerably and was very dependent on the skill of the operators and graders who had assessed the original prints. By the 1990s, printers were fully automatic and no longer required an operator, other than for the purpose of loading and unloading rolls of film and paper. Output had by now risen to 20,000 prints per hour and various technical advances had dramatically reduced the number of reprints required.

The main thrust of the development effort was directed at overcoming the limitations of the "integration to grey" method for controlling the exposures of colour printers. There were a number of factors, some of which were conflicting, which had to be considered.

One major difficulty was the variation between the different types of films and, to a lesser extent, the variation in the film batches. The printing characteristics of Kodak, Fuji and other films are different and there are also variations between 100 ASA films and the faster 400 ASA films. To make matters worse, the printing characteristics of films change with age, storage conditions and the time interval between exposing and developing the film. These were serious problems in the early years, but have become of considerably less concern by the end of the 20th century.

Another consideration, which has to be taken into account with integration to grey, is what is called subject failure. Integration to grey is dependent on there being a reasonable mix of colours in a scene, which is generally the case with outdoor scenes. However, there are many instances when this is not true: for example, a beach scene with large amounts of blue sea and sky. This will fool the printer into trying to correct for the large amount of blue with the result that the print will be far too yellow. Another typical example is a portrait where the colour of the subject's clothes, for example, a bright red sweater, can become the dominant colour and again this would give an incorrect colour balance.

The first attempts to alleviate this, resulted in the so-called "low correction printing" which involved modifying the light which reached the photocells so as to reduce the effect of dominant colours in the scene. While this was effective for certain kinds of scenes, it reduced the ability of the printer to correct for over and underexposed pictures and variations in film batches.

Over the years various refinements were introduced, such as making the photocells read only part of the scene in order to reduce the effect of dominant colours. Further innovations included sensing a large number of sections of an image separately, and using ever more complicated algorithms to compute the exposures required to produce acceptable prints. There is no doubt that the results, in combination with the improvements in film and paper, were considerable.

The Agfa MSP

However, none of these developments eliminated the need to adjust the printers for different films. The printers were provided with a number of pre-set channels which had to be selected depending on the film type. In the early years, photofinishers sorted the films they received by type and selected the appropriate film channel. Later on, DX coding, which identified the type and speed, was added to the films and this enabled both cameras and printers to read the film type. From this, printers were able to select the appropriate channel according to the type of film being printed. This situation continued until 1983 when Agfa introduced their MSP printer, which incorporated what Agfa called TFS (Total Film Scanning). This involves running the whole film past some sensors, which make a series of measurements of all the frames and from this the printing characteristics of the film are deduced and used to set the printer control. With this system, any type of film can be printed without the need to select a preset channel.

The improvements brought about by the Agfa MSP printers were quite dramatic. They made it much easier to produce good quality prints and, at the same time, were very much simpler to set up than their rivals. Some of their competitors, principally Eastman Kodak and Gretag, a Swiss manufacturer, claimed to be able to match their quality and, although this was probably true, their methods required a far greater skill on the part of the photofinisher's quality control staff. This has always been a problem in many processing labs.

In the 1960s and 1970's Kodak's main competitors in the area of processing equipment, and in particular colour printers, were Pako in the US and Agfa. Both companies produced an impressive range of equipment. Kodak relied on their own sales force, as did Agfa, while Pako used dealers and distributors in the US, Europe and Asia. There was a further difference, in that Kodak had a captive market in their own labs and it probably made the work of the other companies even harder as they tried to obtain their share of the independent photofinisher's business.

Pako found that there were not many suitable dealers outside the US and, instead, handed its European distribution over to Gevaert who used it as a tool to market their colour paper and chemicals. There were a number of European photofinishers, who managed to equip substantial processing labs with, what was then quite expensive Pako equipment, financed entirely by their purchases of Gevaert paper. Similarly Agfa, whose policy was not to set up their own labs, financed a number of sizeable photofinishers on the understanding that they would use Agfa materials.

During the early 1960s, colour photography was growing rapidly and all the parties were happy. However, the seeds were sown for some very serious competition, which took place between the major players several years later.

In the sixties and seventies, the main developments concerned colour printers. As the printers improved, attention focused on other aspects. As early as 1959, Technicolor had built a high-speed photofinishing printer for use in what had been the Pavelle Color lab in New York. In order to obtain an output of 5,000 prints per hour, all the films were spliced together in a long roll and automatically fed through the printer. This system was widely adopted in the late 60s, although outputs were more modest. Initially, equipment adapted from the cine industry was used to splice together the films after they had been processed in a dip and dunk processor.

One of the triggers for this development was the introduction of Instamatic (126 size) films in 1963. These were 35 mm wide with a single sprocket hole per frame and this made them particularly suitable for automatic feeding through colour printers. This signalled the rapid decline of 127 and 120 roll films. The introduction of the Pocket Instamatic (110) films in 1972 also accelerated their demise.

Film Formats

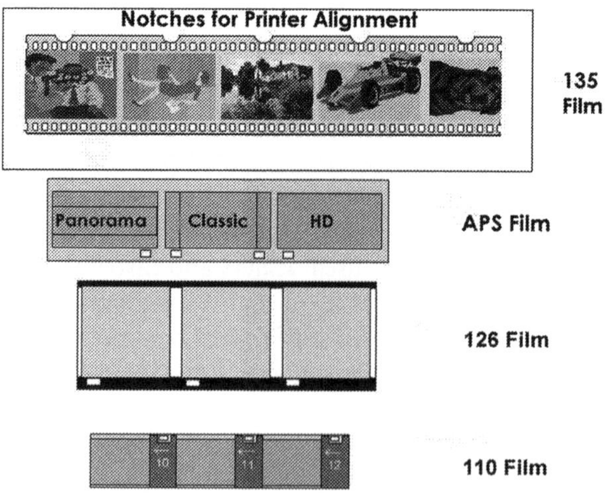

In 35 mm films, the frames are in no fixed position relative to the sprocket holes, and to allow them to be auto-fed through colour printers, several companies, including Agfa and Gretag, developed equipment, which could sense the edge of each frame and then punch a notch into the edge of the film, which would then be detected by the printer.

As the printers improved, it became apparent that uniformity of processing could affect the quality of the negatives and prints. With a dip and dunk processor, the bottom of the film remains in each solution for a longer time than does the top end and hence processing varies over the length of the film. Processors which are used in the cine industry, where long lengths of film are pulled through a series of tanks, provide much more uniform processing.

The next step was therefore to splice together all the 35mm and 126 films received by the lab and then to process them on a cine-type processor.

Initially this pre-splicing had to be carried out in the dark and was quite slow, perhaps working at a rate of only 20–30 films per hour. In addition to splicing, the films had to be identified so that the films and prints could be returned to the correct customer. As we have seen, Barker had already encountered this problem in the 1920s. Various methods have since been used to solve the problem, including photographing the number from the dealer envelope onto the end of each film, or printing a bar code on the splice and film bag.

Over the years much improved splicers have been produced, and they are now completely automatic. This automation includes extracting the film from the cassette. The splicers can also be operated in daylight. The latest models are alleged to handle up to 500 films per hour, but this is probably a little optimistic. The splicers place a roll of several hundred films in a light tight cassette, which fits onto the daylight-operating, cine-type, processing machine.

In the early days of printing onto roll paper, the processed rolls were cut into individual prints by means of a hand guillotine. As volumes increased, this produced a bottleneck, so Pako, Kodak and others designed automatic cutters to chop up the rolls. The cutters were able to sense a mark on the paper, which had been put there at the printing stage. Various different types of marks have been used, including graphite or ink on the back of the paper, or small holes or slots punched between prints, which are then cut away by the cutter.

The Fully Mechanised Lab – The Picture Factory

This method of cutting up the rolls of prints automatically was a big step forward, but as the film processing and printing methods improved, the remainder of the process which consisted of sorting, pricing and packaging the negatives and prints, became an ever bigger burden. This will become clear as we now begin to follow a film through the whole process of a photofinishing lab.

When we take a film to a shop, it is usually put into an envelope on which is printed a number and barcode. This identifies the shop and provides an order number. The envelope is then marked by the shopkeeper with the type of film and the type of service that is required by the customer, i.e. the number and size of prints required. The customer is then given a tear-off portion as a receipt. The envelopes are usually collected from the shop once or twice a day. Many shops now offer an overnight service, which means that the photofinisher has only a few hours in which to develop and print the film before it is delivered back to the shop.

On arrival at the photofinisher the envelopes are sorted by film type and order details and the films are sent for splicing, ready for processing. The splicer prints a number or bar code on both the envelope and the film. The envelopes are stored in sequence.

After processing, the roll of spliced films is printed and the roll of exposed paper is processed. We are now left with a pile of envelopes, a roll of perhaps 200 films and a roll of say 5,000 prints, some of which are not correct and will need reprinting. So that the prints can be matched up with the films, the photographic printer makes an additional mark on the roll of prints showing the beginning and end of each order. Depending on how the lab is organised, these procedures will so far have taken 2-3 hours.

The next stage is for an operator to check the prints while they are still on the roll. The usual procedure is to mark faulty prints with a china graph, either with a cross if they are to be scrapped, or a correction if they are to be reprinted. There are now a variety of packaging machines available for the next stages. The actual sequences may vary a little, but the principle is the same.

The roll of films and prints are loaded onto the packaging machine, which cuts the films into short strips and the paper roll into individual prints. The print cutter contains a sorter which senses the china graph marks and separates the prints from each film into the good prints (which have no marks), the scrapped prints and those which require reprinting. In the case of films where all the prints are good, or at least acceptable, the prints and strips of films are then inserted into a wallet and an outer envelope on which is printed the original shop identification barcode.

Sometimes the original envelope is re-used. A similar procedure will apply where there are scrapped prints, but when no prints are to be reprinted. At the same time, the number of prints in the order will have been counted and a label printed which indicates the retail price.

Work Flow in Typical Wholesale Lab

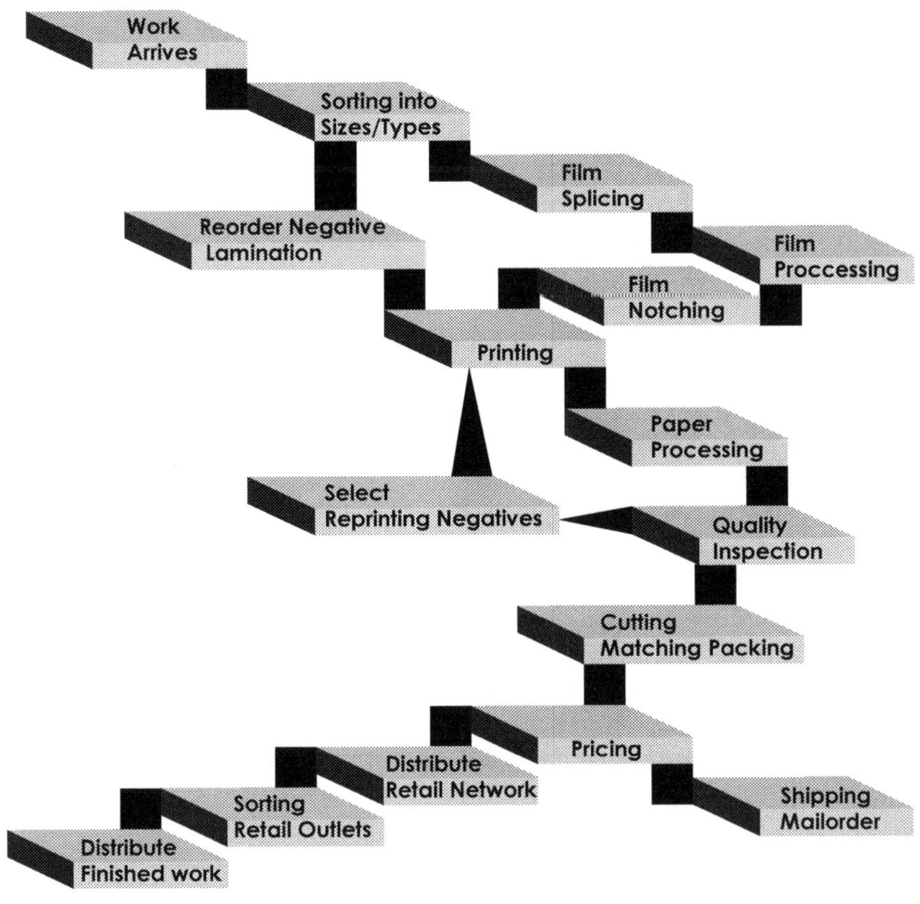

The real complication is caused by those pictures which have to be reprinted. The packaging machine separates the films and prints which do not require reprinting and are ready for despatch, from those where some pictures need to be reprinted. The latter are then taken back to a colour printer, the negatives are identified, and the correction, which has been specified by the print checker, is then keyed into the printer and a further print is made. When it has been processed, the new print is checked and, if satisfactory, is cut and packed with the other good prints into a wallet and envelope, for return to the shop.

The precise method of handling these remakes varies from lab to lab. In many cases this function is carried out by a minilab. However, there are other systems where the strips of negatives to be reprinted are laminated to a plastic band and run automatically through specially equipped colour printers. Another system reprints the appropriate negatives before the rolls of films are cut, identifying them by counting the number of prints from the start of the order up to the china graph marks.

As the volume of films has increased and also as a result of competition, service times have become shorter and the cutting, sorting, pricing and packaging part of the whole process has become very critical. We have come a long way since the first print cutters, a pair of scissors for cutting the films into strips and large numbers of people, mostly women, who did the sorting and packing by hand.

For many years, when most of the retail prices were the same, the envelopes were stamped with the number of prints and the price. The trade associations used to sell rubber stamps for this. Once this cosy situation came to an end, the photofinishers were forced to mark each order with the retailer's price, which might vary from week to week or even from branch to branch. As a result, elaborate pricing computers, connected to the finisher's accounting system, which produce the delivery notes, invoices and statistics are now standard in all large labs.

This area of photofinishing gradually employed an ever larger proportion of the total lab staff, until it had reached over 30% by the 1970s. This percentage is now much lower as some of the latest packaging machines are almost completely automatic, with one person tending several machines. Many of these can handle 400–500 orders per hour compared to perhaps 30–50 per hour in the days of manual sorting and packaging.

The cost of remaking prints also became an important factor in hastening improvements to colour printers. There are various estimates, depending on how "creative" one's accounting methods are, suggesting that a remake costs 5–10 times as much as a first- time print. Naturally, the number of first-time acceptable prints depends, not only on the technology and competence of the staff, but also on the quality which one is aiming to achieve. With the very best printers and processors, set up correctly, remakes may be as low as 1–2 %. On the other hand, in very quality-conscious markets, such as Germany or Switzerland, there were times in the sixties and seventies, when the top photofinishers were reprinting as many as 70% - 80% of all negatives. As we collect our prints from the shop, we might speculate on how quality-conscious the photofinishers think we are.

There is yet a further stage after packaging and pricing the orders. A large lab, processing anything from 2–10 million films per annum, may have to handle between 20,000 and 100,000 orders on its busiest days, many within 4–6 hours of receipt. The completed orders have to be sorted by the addresses of the retailers who sent them and placed into boxes or bags ready for delivery. It is an operation which is not very different from that of a post office and indeed, similar developments in the sorting function have taken place within both industries. In the early years, when most labs were considerably smaller than today, sorting was a manual operation but nowadays many labs use very large, automatic sorters.

A more recent development has been concerned with sorting films when they first arrive at the lab. Each retailer will be sending a "mixed bag" consisting of mostly colour negative films, some black and white, some colour transparencies and perhaps orders for enlargements and further prints. These have to be sorted, sometimes logged in to make sure they are not lost and then transported to the appropriate department or pre-splicer. This was, and still is, a very labour-intensive operation, but a few of the largest labs have, in recent years, installed sorters, complete with conveyor systems, to carry out the process.

The Maxilab

Over the years, there have been many attempts to automate various parts of the photofinishing operation, not only to cut costs, but also to speed up the processes involved. One of the most stunning, at least in appearance, is the Maxilab, which was produced by GPE, a subsidiary of a large Italian photofinisher.

In a traditional lab, after each stage, that is after the pre-splicer, the film processor, the colour printer, the roll paper processor and finally the print checker, the film and paper are spooled up and the rolls transferred manually to the next stage. The Maxilab omits spooling up the rolls and directly connects the film or paper to the next stage. While it certainly speeds up the work using what appears to be an elegant system, in practice it is not quite so straightforward. The complication is due to the fact that the splicers, processors and printers operate at different speeds and, in order to solve this, the Maxilab has massive, adjustable-length, storage loops between its sections. A very complicated control system stops and starts the various parts, so as to make the whole lab run at a constant speed. It works quite well provided that the lab has a large and relatively even flow of work such as a mail-order lab.

Conversely, it becomes difficult to keep it running in a lab with an intermittent arrival of work. Although developed in the eighties, there are relatively few installations still working now.

Coupled Printer Processors

Much more successful than the Maxilab, have been Agfa's coupled printer processors, the MSPs and its later development, the Dymax printer, both of which can make up to 20,000 prints per hour, and can either spool up the paper in a roll, or better still, can be coupled to a VSP (variable speed processor). The processor has a series of tanks containing the solutions through which the roll of paper is transported over and under rollers at the top and bottom of the tanks. In most processors the top and bottom rollers are fixed and are driven at a constant speed, so as to keep the time that the paper is in the various solutions constant. In the Agfa VSP processor, the bottom rollers can be raised, thereby shortening the length of the loops of paper. As the bottom rollers are raised, the drive speed is reduced so that the time that the paper is in the solutions is kept constant. By this means, the processor speed adjusts itself between 10 and 50 metres per minute and, with only a small storage conveyor, the processor can remain coupled to the printer. If the printer stops for any length of time, the printer and processor are disconnected. Gretag and, possibly, other printers have since been adapted to couple to the Agfa VSP.

The Disc Films and Cameras

There were two other events in the history of photofinishing which have had a profound effect on the industry. In 1982, Kodak launched its disc films and cameras, which could not be processed or printed using existing equipment. The negatives were much smaller: 8 x11mm, compared to 24 x 36mm for a 35 mm film and instead of being in a strip, were fixed like petals, on the periphery of a small plastic disc.

Kodak demonstrated to the industry a set of printing and processing equipment they had designed and invited other manufacturers to produce their own versions, offering licences for their numerous patents.

The films were in a light tight cassette, which had to be broken open. The films were then threaded onto a spindle. Processing was carried out by placing the spindles horizontally on a rack and transporting them through a series of shallow tanks in a manner similar to a dip and dunk processor. The spindles were positioned just above the tanks and rotated so as to dip the films into the solutions. The film processors could be built in a number of ways, from high-output automatic versions, to much simpler semi-manual models.

Although many of the printers of the time could be adapted to handle the negatives, fully automatic printing at high speed required new models, which only one company was prepared to produce. By the time it was ready, it had become clear that disc films were not the success that Kodak had hoped for and it was never put into production.

APS – The Advanced Photo System

Of far greater importance was the Advanced Photo System introduced in 1996. The 24 mm wide films which, in addition to the emulsion, had a transparent magnetic coating on the back, were placed in a new type of cassette with a number of very specific features. From a photofinishing point of view, the fact that the cassettes were serial numbered and that, after processing, the films were returned to the customer in the original cassette, created a major complication.

The problem is that, at the pre-splicing stage, after the films have been removed, the cassettes need to be stored in sequence. After printing, the films have to be re-inserted into their correct cassettes and packed with their prints. To achieve this for a lab handling 5–10,000 APS films per day, requires some very complicated machinery.

Colour printing from APS films is not too difficult, but the printers require some fitments so that they can automatically carry out the instructions coded on to the magnetic coating of the film. These include selecting one of three print sizes as well as printing various pieces of information on to the back of the prints.

The companies who produced the APS system stipulated that the photofinishers should provide an Index print with each processed film. This is a print with up to 20 postage stamp-sized pictures, one for each frame of the film, and each numbered so as to make re-ordering easier. Various methods were used to produce these but most involved making a low-resolution scan of the film and printing them either on a separate printer or, latterly, on the same roll of paper as the prints. Index prints have proved to be very popular and many photofinishers also provide them for 35mm as well as APS films.

Initially the industry produced low-output attachments for minilabs and a considerable amount of time elapsed before high-volume photofinishers were properly equipped. Not least was the matter of cost, which was in excess of $1,000,000 per lab. Not many photofinishers were prepared to invest such a sum until it had been proved that the sales of cameras and films would justify this.

The industry was faced with a classic "catch 22" situation. It was difficult to sell APS cameras and films until processing was readily available, but the photofinishing industry was reluctant to install the equipment until there were enough films to justify the investment. Although five companies were involved in the development of APS, Kodak had the most at stake. They broke the deadlock by equipping each of their many labs worldwide and, for a year or more, provided a service to the rest of the industry.

One of the, not so widely publicised, aims of the APS system, was to try to increase the profitability of photofinishing, which had been suffering from cut-throat competition. The hope was that consumers could be persuaded to buy APS cameras because of their various easy-to-use features and then would be prepared to pay premium prices for their prints. To a certain extent this has happened, but whether the higher photofinishing prices have compensated for the large investment required, is not clear.

So far our account of photofinishing up to the Millennium has concentrated on colour negative film and prints, which comprise well over 90% of the total. There have, however, been some developments in the developing and printing of black and white films and also in the processing of colour transparencies.

Black & White

By the beginning of the 1960s, black and white methods had diverged between, on one side, the US and the UK, who were using roll printers, and on the other, the more quality-conscious countries, such as Germany and Japan, who were printing onto sheet paper using several contrast grades to match the different types of negatives. This changed as Agfa and several other European manufacturers developed paper whose contrast could be altered by pre-flashing. In this method, prior to exposing the negative, the whole of the area to be printed is given a very short exposure of white light, which is not sufficient to produce a visible image. The effect of this pre-flash is to increase the contrast of the paper. By varying the intensity of the pre-flash, several degrees of contrast are possible.

Agfa and several other manufacturers introduced roll printers, which automatically pre-flashed the paper before making the exposure. The operator could select the degree of pre-flashing and hence the contrast most suited to the negative which was to be printed.

By the end of the 20th Century, the proportion of black and white films had become fairly small. However, many people who take black and white pictures are very demanding of quality. Consequently, many of the larger photofinishers have stopped developing black and white films and are contracting out the work to specialist B&W labs.

Slide or Transparency Films

There have also been a number of changes in the processing of colour transparencies. For many of the earlier years, Kodachrome was the transparency of choice for discerning photographers, which, with the exception of a few labs in the US and, for a short time, one lab in the UK, was always processed by Kodak. After World War 2, a few other manufacturers brought out transparency films, which could be processed by independent photofinishers. In addition, Kodak introduced Ektachrome films for processing by independent labs, but these were aimed more at professional photographers. For some years this created a very fragmented situation, as most films required different processing methods. The situation continued until the late 1970s, when most manufacturers including, Agfa, Fuji and Konica had made their films compatible with Kodak's E6 Ektachrome process. Since then, photofinishers have been able to offer a single process for all makes of transparencies. However, due to the ever-decreasing market share, only a few labs now process transparencies, while the rest contract out the work.

There has always been a demand for prints from transparencies, but for most of the time it has been relatively small, as the majority of snap-shooters require prints from colour negative film. Following the success of Pavelle Color in New York during the 1950s using Ansco Printon material, there have been several different methods of production.

Eastman Kodak also offered a service using a material similar to Printon, but this was never released to independent photofinishers.

For some years Kodak provided a special film, which was used by the labs to make a negative from the transparency and this was then printed with the other work. The advantage of this method was that very little additional equipment was required, although it did involve considerable extra work. Another disadvantage was that, unless great care was taken, the prints were degraded in comparison with the original.

From the late 1960s Kodak, followed a few years later by Agfa and Fuji, provided reversal paper for printing without an intermediate negative and this was widely used until the late 1990s. Printing was relatively simple, but the disadvantage was that the reversal paper required different processing and hence additional machinery from that needed for the paper which was used to print from negatives.

In 1986 Agfa demonstrated a scanner and an electronic printer, which avoided the need for an intermediate negative and which printed onto the same type of colour paper as was used for printing from negatives. When the equipment was introduced a few years later, it had an output of 1000 prints per hour, which was adequate for most labs. Unfortunately it was fairly expensive, so it was not taken up by many of the labs that were equipped for printing onto reversal paper. However, by 2001, digital minilabs had become very widespread and the same method as had been pioneered by Agfa, has been widely adopted ever since; so much so that, by 2003, most manufacturers had announced that they were discontinuing the supply of reversal paper.

Professional Photofinishing

As we have seen, amateur photofinishing, the developing and printing of amateur photographs during the first 80 years of the 20th century, changed from a craft activity to a highly mechanised industrial process. In the early years of the century its methods differed little from those used by professional photographers except, that the latter having used studio cameras and glass plates, generally made larger prints which were finished to a higher standard. The differences became more pronounced with the growth of colour prints during the 1950s.

At the end of that decade, some amateurs were able to produce quite acceptable colour prints of social events, such as weddings, while many professional photographers either could not, or the costs were so high, that very few clients were able or willing to pay for hand-made colour prints.

In the early 1960s photofinishers installed equipment to make 5"x7" and 8"x10" prints and some social photographers started to offer machine made colour prints. This was not ideal, partly because many photographers had always relied on a certain amount of cropping in the darkroom and this was not so easy with machine made prints. On the other hand, photofinishers, geared up for amateur work, were not set up to produce work to standards that professional photographers could sell at an acceptable price. This resulted in several trends.

In some countries, particularly France, Germany and Italy, the larger photofinishers started separate professional departments to serve the social photographers doing wedding, portrait and schools work. The techniques were similar to amateur photofinishing, except that much more care was taken and frequently most of the negatives were printed twice, a test print followed by a final print. A few labs, mainly in the US, provided a degree of negative cropping. This was done by supplying the photographers with several different sized cards each with a different size of aperture. The photographers mounted their negatives on to the cards with the appropriate apertures so that the labs could print the section of the negatives which the photographers had selected.

For some years this type of professional finishing was reasonably successful. However, the fundamental problem was the difference in philosophy required for amateur and professional photofinishing. Amateur photofinishing is a business which has always aimed to produce high-quality pictures through the use of technology. Professionally taken pictures have always required much more craft work, whether it was for judging colour balance, print spotting or mounting. As a result there has been a split of the two types of business.

Over the years separate professional photofinishing labs started. Most of these were concerned with social photographers, some specialised in wedding, others in portrait or schools photography, each of which require slightly different expertise.

By the mid 1960s there had been another development. A number of manufacturers, mainly in the UK, France, Germany and Italy introduced scaled-down versions of photofinishing equipment, which were particularly suitable for producing machine-made colour prints in moderate quantities. As a result, some of the larger social photographers opened their own labs.

Typical of these was the Pavelle brothers' English company, Pavelle Ltd., which manufactured a range of printers, film and paper processors very suited to this market. Other manufacturers of this type of equipment were Priox in France, Müllersohn in Germany, San Marco, Safai and Italfoto in Italy. Particularly prominent was Pavelle Ltd, which in September 1970 became part of the Italian enlarger manufacturer Durst. From about 1965 they produced over 10,000 professional printers including their Miniprinter, which when it was launched cost about £500, a fraction of the cost of a photofinishing printer, and helped to switch social photography to colour.

A good example of the effect of this type of low-volume photofinishing equipment, was P & F James, who were wedding photographers in west London. In 1965 they installed a Pavelle printer and processor and found that they could produce colour prints for less than black and white prints and consequently switched over to colour without any increase in prices. The reason was quite simple; the black and white prints were hand-enlarged in a darkroom, whereas colour was produced in full daylight on automatic equipment. Their biggest change in working practices was to make sure that all their pictures were accurately composed in the camera, making them suitable for machine printing. Within two years, the majority of UK social photographers had changed to colour and the situation was similar in other countries.

Video Analyser

An interesting development took place in the US. In 1967 Alex Dreyfoos and George Mergens, who had previously worked for Pavelle Color in New York, produced a video colour negative analyser (VCNA). On inserting a colour negative, the analyser displayed an enlarged positive on a TV screen. Four calibrated dials allowed the operator to adjust the brightness and colour of the picture until he, or she, was satisfied with its appearance. The readings of the dials were then used to set the exposure time and colour filtration of the printer or enlarger. Depending on how critical the work was, it enabled some labs to produce many first-time prints, or for very critical work reduce three or four test prints to one. The VCNA was marketed by Kodak and many were installed in professional photofinishing works. By today's standards, the VCNA does not sound very startling. However, in 1967 and for many years, it was quite an achievement. The trick and difficulty was to match the characteristics of the VCNA to that of the negative and colour paper so that applying the readings of the dials, would provide the correct filtration and exposures to produce good prints.

Resin Coated Paper

A further development, which indirectly affected photofinishing occurred in 1971. At the end of the 1960s Kodak launched Resin Coated (RC) colour paper. Instead of coating the emulsion on a paper base, the paper was first covered with a thin layer of Polyethylene and the emulsions were coated on top of this waterproof layer. The purpose was to stop the processing chemicals soaking into the base from which they had to be removed by several chemical processes and prolonged washing. This enabled Kodak to simplify the process from five to three stages, plus a much reduced wash, thereby reducing the time from half an hour to less than ten minutes. RC paper greatly reduced the size of processing machines for a given output, not to mention a considerable reduction in water and energy consumption.

This RC paper, as it was called, was a great improvement, as long as it was processed in a high-speed photofinishing processor. For some inexplicable reason, Kodak appeared to have overlooked the fact that many professional labs and photographers processed colour paper in batches. Interaction of the developer and bleach-fix occurs when transferring the paper from the developer to the bleach-fix tank and this often caused staining or streaking. There was an easy cure for this, adding an extra stage into the process, which was both inexpensive and non-critical. Eastman Kodak, who by this time had a reputation for arrogance, said "No" and left their professional customers to struggle.

A solution, which was acceptable to Kodak and their professional customers, was produced by Dwight Krehbil, who introduced the Kreonite roller transport processor in 1971. Dwight, a very ingenious designer, who had started his career as a photographer with Boeing in Witchita, Kansas, had struggled to make his mark with a series of very innovative but commercially unsuccessful products and for years had been treated as an eccentric "nut case" by the rest of the industry, suddenly became a hero. He produced a mechanism which would transport both single sheets and long rolls of colour paper through the four tanks required to process RC paper. The system squeegeed the surface of the paper when it passed from tank to tank and this stopped the staining and streaking.

The machine was ingenious, its rollers were covered by a Nylon sock which collapsed or expanded as the paper passed over them, thereby altering their circumference so as to transport long lengths of paper without excessive tension. Up to that time roller transport processors had only been used for single sheets of X-ray or graphic arts film. Another interesting feature of the Kreonite processor was how it was manufactured. It contained a large number of very complex shaped parts made of chemical resistant materials. To machine these would have been very expensive and would have made the processors unaffordable. The alternative was to injection-mould the parts, but the cost of the tools would have been enormous, considering the fact that only a few hundred machines were likely to be required each year.

Dwight developed a very simple method for making moulding tools in a few hours compared to the hundreds of hours that it normally took. Even the prototype machine, which had several hundred different parts, consisted entirely of injection-moulded components. There were several further advantages, all the parts were interchangeable and could be assembled by relatively unskilled staff and, furthermore, every machine was identical. At that time injection moulding was not widely used for photofinishing equipment and building processing machines was a skilled task. Frequently the performance of individual machines depended on who had built them. Although there are now other methods of making moulding tools quickly, as far as is known, no other manufacturer of complicated low-volume capital equipment, in any industry, has ever used injection moulding to such an extent as Kreonite. The processors were produced until 2003 and were very similar to those introduced more than 30 years ago.

It took other manufacturers, such as Hope, San Marco, Colenta and Hostert, who were craft based, more than two years to produce properly functioning roller transport colour paper processors.

This brings us to the end of the 20th century, by which time photofinishing had moved from craft-based to a highly automated industry. However, for the last twenty years of that time there has been a return to retail processing in the form of minilabs and more recently the advent of electronic photography and digital technology.

1 Coote Jack H. Photofinishing Techniques, Focal Press 1970 P16–17

2 Coote Jack H. Photofinishing Techniques, Focal Press 1970 P18

3 Ptt, F.H. G. & Selwyn, E.W.H. "Colour of Outdoor Photographic Subjects" Photographic Journal March 1938, Vol.78 pp 115–21

CHAPTER 4

Minilabs

Photofinishing, like so many other things in life, goes round and round in circles. At the end of the 19th century, before George Eastman set up his processing works in Rochester and Harrow, those photographers who did not want to do their own developing and printing, would have their plates or films developed and printed by the local photo shop. The number of serious amateur photographers and snap-shooters grew and later, with the advent of colour, the photo shops started to send the work out to specialist photofinishing labs so that by the 1960s there were very few retailers doing processing on the premises. Furthermore, the photofinishers, anxious to extend their business, started supplying other types of retailer such as drug stores, supermarkets and tourist shops, so that by the 1970s there was an enormous choice of places where one could take or send one's films for processing. From the 1980s the situation has been moving back towards the earlier situation and many retail shops have once more arranged to do developing and printing on the premises.

So what has caused these changes? In the first place the increase in the number of films, plus the complexity of colour, made it impracticable to carry out processing in the back of a shop. Furthermore photofinishers, with their mechanised equipment, could do the work far more cheaply and shopkeepers preferred to take in films for developing and printing, without all the hassle of doing the work..

Several other things were also happening. Colour processing required far greater investment in equipment than many photofinishers in the late 1950s and 1960s were able or willing to make. This resulted in mergers and, in the US, several photofinishers went public in order to raise additional capital on the stock market. These mergers were further encouraged by the growth of the pharmacy, drug store and discount retailer chains, who were looking for larger suppliers.

The standard of work done by the wholesale photofinishers was, to say the least, variable and it was difficult to know where to take one's precious film in order to be sure that the results would be excellent. To be fair to photofinishers doing colour in the 1960s, part of the problem lay with the colour films of the day, which tended to vary from batch to batch and the way in which they had been stored. Some of this could be compensated for in the printing, but this required time and skills, which were not always available to finishers handling a large number of films to a deadline determined by their delivery schedules and constrained by the low prices demanded by their retailers. This created the potential demand for a service which would be more dependable.

During the sixties and seventies, several European manufacturers, principally Pavelle Ltd in the UK, San Marco, Safai and Italfoto in Italy, produced small-scale photofinishing equipment, which, from an output and cost point of view, would have been suitable for the retail processing of colour films. The printers and processors were scaled-down versions of those used by larger photofinishers, but that did not make them suitable for use inside a retail shop. They occupied more space, not to mention services, than most shops could provide but, more importantly, they required considerable technical expertise in order to produce consistently good quality.

This type of equipment was suitable for the technically-minded owner manager who was able to devote most of his time to operating it, hardly a formula for running a successful retail shop. As we have seen, these mini-photofinishing labs worked very well for professional photographers or small professional labs who had the expertise and also were able to charge considerably more for their pictures than for amateur snapshots. No doubt some professional photographers, especially in France and Italy, where many had retail premises and had traditionally developed amateur black and white films, did some developing and printing of amateur colour films in the 1970s, but it was not the kind of retail photofinishing that we now associate with minilabs.

One of the important features of successful retail photofinishing equipment is that it can be operated in daylight and that the paper processor is coupled to the printer, eliminating the need for the operator to transfer the paper from the printer to the processor. Interestingly, the Pavelle Corporation demonstrated such a device at an exhibition in New York in 1961. Dr Kurt Jacobson, head of Pavelle's English company had produced colour paper which could be processed with only two chemical steps in less than ten minutes, compared to other colour papers of that time which required four or five chemicals and took about 30 minutes to process. They demonstrated the process with the P100 printer processor designed by Alex Dreyfoos and George Mergens, who later became better known for the VCNA (Video Color Negative Analyser) marketed by Kodak. The P100, about the size of a slide projector, operated in daylight, printing onto a roll of 3½" wide paper. After each negative had been exposed, the paper was cut and the exposed frame transported through a miniature processing machine containing the two solutions, developer and bleach-fix. The colour prints dropped into a tray about three minutes later. This was only a demonstrator for the rapid process colour paper and did not include wash tanks and a dryer. It took another decade and a half before a Japanese manufacturer produced a fully engineered printer processor suitable for use in a retail shop. The P100 printer processor incorporated colour and exposure measurements and the results were stunning. The story goes that Kodak brought a planeload of their scientists to see the demonstration and this acted as a catalyst for their R&D efforts to shorten and simplify their colour paper process.

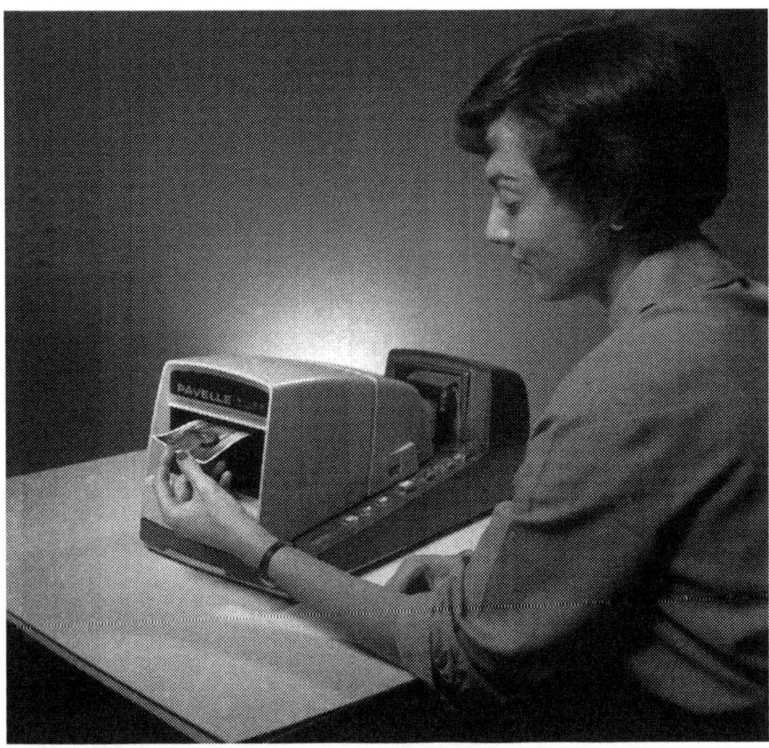

Pavelle P100 Printer-Processor

The first true attempt to introduce retail colour photofinishing was probably made by Pako in the mid 1970s[1]. They set up test sites to do retail processing in Minneapolis and Fort Lauderdale using what were essentially the printers and processors that they supplied to their larger photofinisher customers. The idea was to provide a very fast on-site service at a premium price.

The success of the test sites led to the establishment of a franchise program by a company in Boston. After selling several franchises and helping to get them started they were convinced that on-site retail processing was the way forward. However, they realised it would require special equipment. Unfortunately the new Chief Operations Officer at Pako, who had been recruited from outside the industry, did not recognise this market and the necessary equipment was therefore not developed. There was considerable turmoil in the company over this and also over several other ideas and some of the senior executives left Pako. It probably spelt the beginning of the end for one of the world's greatest equipment manufacturers and a sad memorial to Glen Dye, the founder, who for over 50 years had innovated many of the techniques used in the industry, some of which are still in use to this day.

Noritsu

The big breakthrough came in 1976 when Noritsu who, at that time, were hardly known outside Japan, showed a completely different type of equipment specifically designed for retail photofinishing. The equipment was very compact and could be operated in daylight, making it suitable for use in a retail shop. It consisted of a film processor and a combined printer processor, which could develop and print films in one hour. The printer processor also cut the prints and sorted the orders, making it relatively simple to operate.

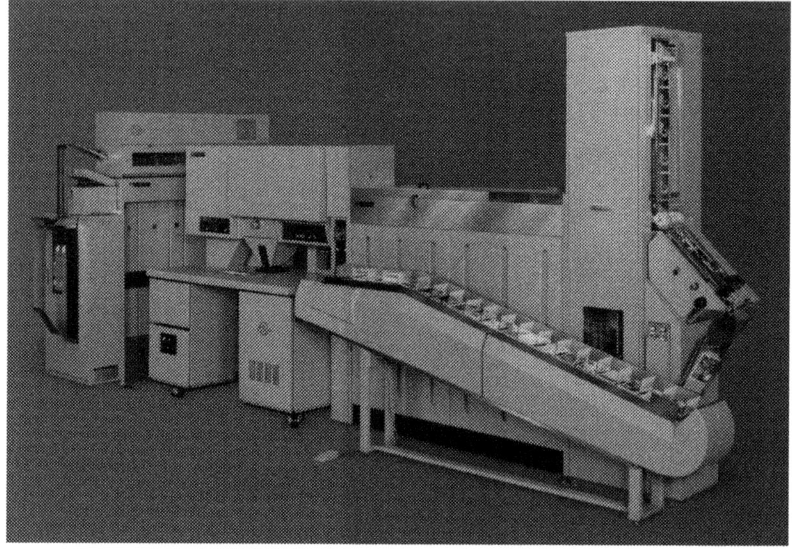

Noritsu QSS-2 Minilab 1979

The Noritsu minilab, as it came to be called, was fairly expensive. Provided it was in a suitable location to attract enough work, it produced good quality and charged a premium price for a one or two hour service, it could produce a very satisfactory return for the owner. Operation was reasonably straightforward and most intelligent people, with a modicum of mechanical aptitude, could learn how to operate it successfully quite quickly. Probably the most difficult thing to master was colour correction. Although by the time Noritsu introduced its minilab, colour printers were fairly good at printing a wide range of negatives, manual correction was still required for several prints of each order. In addition, considerable perseverance, care and attention to detail were essential in order to produce a good quality consistently. Noritsu were probably motivated by the fact that in Japan there were many extremely well run small colour labs, where the willingness to concentrate on good quality was taken for granted. This was by no means universal in North America and some parts of Europe.

Photography has always attracted enterprising people from other walks of life and Minilabs certainly did that. In the first instance they were of two kinds. There were a number of people who had a little capital and were keen to start their own business. The other were successful professionals, doctors, dentists, accountants and lawyers, who in many cases themselves were keen amateur photographers, and fancied the idea of investing in their own processing lab, but employing others to run it.

Many of the first minilabs were set up as free-standing operations only offering D&P and selling films, albums, frames and possibly a few simple cameras. The idea of a minilab as part of a much larger shop, which sold other goods, came later.

For the first few years, growth was comparatively slow; there were a number of installations in Japan followed by some in California and thereafter in the rest of the USA as well as several places in Europe. Soon other Japanese manufacturers, principally Copal, followed by Konica and Fuji, had introduced minilabs. At first there was considerable scepticism about whether these minilabs could really produce adequate quality and, particularly in Europe, doubts as to whether they were viable. This is not surprising when one considers the cost and other characteristics of minilabs in the late 1970s and how this changed over the next twenty years.

In the early 1980s a number of photofinishers, afraid that free-standing minilabs might take away some of their business, tried installing minilabs in their customers shops, but this did not work very well. Apart from the high costs, the expertise required to operate the minilabs was too great for retail staff, who were very rarely dedicated craftsmen. Simplifying the operation to overcome this took at least a decade.

Minilabs have made enormous strides in both performance and cost-effectiveness since that time. There were a number of technical advances and the quality produced by most minilabs has improved considerably. In particular, digital minilabs, compared to the machines of the late 1970s, are able to produce a far greater range of work . A good illustration of the cost advances can be seen from some figures for Noritsu minilabs, which were sold in the UK.

Year	**1979**	**2002**
Model	QSS-2	QSS-3001
Output 3½"x 5" prints per hour	1,069	1,160
Floor area square metres	7.6	2.2
UK cost in GBP	£160,000	£83,000

During that period, inflation reduced the value of the UK currency by a factor of about 3.[2] This suggests a drop in costs in real terms of about 6:1. No doubt the situation in other countries was of a similar order, although as a result of different rates of currency exchange, there will have been variations.

These prices for the capital cost of minilabs need to be looked at in relation to the cost of prints. In monetary terms these have not changed very much. Within the UK, a typical retail price for a colour print, produced by a wholesale photofinisher, both in the late 1970s and in 2002, was about £0.10.[1] Due to the novelty of one hour services in the late 1970s, minilabs were able to charge a substantial premium, possibly of the order of 3-4 times, but competition has reduced this considerably over the period. By 2004 many minilabs were charging no more than retailers who were using wholesale labs.

KIS

In the early days of the 1980's, KIS, a French manufacturer of key cutting equipment, introduced a very simple minilab, which on account of its low cost aroused considerable interest. To those with no experience of colour processing, it appeared to offer the opportunity of jumping on the minilab bandwagon with very much lower investment than that required for the Japanese machines. Apart from the rather primitive construction of its film and paper processors, it dispensed with automatic colour control for the printer, leaving the operator to adjust the colour filters manually. While this might have been suitable for printing studio portraits, it was most unsuitable for amateur snapshots. Several thousand small shopkeepers in the US, UK and France believed that this was a relatively easy way to enter a lucrative market and Installed a KIS minilab. Often however, they discovered that colour processing was not as simple as they had imagined, and found it difficult or even impossible to recover their investment, let alone make a return on it. This incident left the industry, which had always enjoyed an excellent reputation for looking after its customers, rather critical towards this newcomer.

An interesting side-effect of the KIS minilab, which has had long-term effects, occurred in Japan. The KIS minilabs used European colour paper and a shortened chemical process of their own formulation. When KIS introduced them to Japan in the middle of the 1980s, Fuji saw this as a threat to their dominant market position and switched their design and development efforts to minilabs and shortly afterwards stopped producing high-speed photofinishing printers. Fuji launched a succession of minilabs with much improved performance and 15-20 years later dominated the market in several countries.

[1]*Prices from different outlets vary considerably but £0.10 is probably a reasonable average*

It soon became clear that rather the opposite approach to the KIS type of equipment was required. High-quality output, without the need for skilled technicians, was of prime importance and all the reputable manufacturers brought out a succession of models, each one simplifying the operation. Most crucial was the method of setting up the colour printer to cope with the different types of colour negative films and the system of colour measurement required to increase the number of first-time prints. Most adopted multiple-point measurements, with very sophisticated algorithms to calculate the correct exposures and colour filtration. By the early 1990s minilabs had reached a very high standard and several other manufacturers had entered the market.

Copal withdrew from the US and European markets, but manufactured Kodak branded equipment and supplied the processors for Agfa minilabs.

Konica Nice Print System

In July 1984, Konica, who are one of the oldest photographic companies, released the "Nice Print System" [3] a washless process, which did not require the films and prints to be washed with running water which had been the norm until then. The washing stages were replaced by a short chemical process called super stabiliser. This was of considerable importance for retail minilabs, as it was no longer necessary to connect them to a water supply and drain, which meant they could be installed anywhere and easily moved. Most other manufacturers quickly followed their example.

Gretag, who had been very successful with high-speed photofinishing printers, entered the market with an extremely compact machine, dubbed a microlab. This coupled the film processor to the printer processor, so all that the operator had to do was to load the films and the machine did the rest. This helped them to obtain a very substantial share of the "on-site" processing market in the US during the 1990s.

Hope, a leading US manufacturer of professional, graphic arts and X-ray processors, made a big effort to produce minilabs which would be suitable for professional work as well as for amateur photofinishing. They never succeeded in getting the equipment to work sufficiently well to compete with the Japanese manufacturers. As a consequence of concentrating all their efforts on minilabs they neglected their core roller transport processor business and within a few years the company collapsed.

Several European manufacturers made similar attempts, but none apart from Gretag, and to a very much lesser extent their associate San Marco, had any success.

On-site Processing

In the US, drug store, discount and supermarket chains have for many years taken in photofinishing. Having seen the success of the free-standing minilabs, combined with the fact that improved equipment had made it possible to produce acceptable results with moderately skilled staff, they decided to enter the retail photofinishing market in a big way. In addition to being a business in its own right, it provided a way of bringing customers to the store.

Operation of the in-store service presented many challenges and most chains opted to contract it out to the wholesale photofinishers who were providing the normal overnight service. The largest network was that operated by Qualex, Eastman Kodak's photofinishing subsidiary, which operated more than 10,000 minilabs inside their customer's stores. Qualex put in place a sizeable organisation with large numbers of depots all over the US in order to deliver all the materials, service the equipment and train the staff. The Qualex on-site labs, as they are called, were offered on a leasing basis charged by the "click", i.e., the number of prints made. This saved the retailers a large capital investment and the need to put in place an expensive support organisation. Prices for the use of the minilabs were set so that retailers processed the one-hour work in the stores and sent the remainder, about half of the total, to the overnight labs whose costs were considerably lower. For many years this worked very well and, until the Millennium, both parts of the business continued to grow.

One of the attractions for the retailer was having a business, which kept the customers in the store for at least an hour, and in many instances the processing counter is prominently located in the centre of, or near the entrance to, the store. A side-effect of large numbers of mass marketers offering on-site processing has been to lower the cost of one-hour processing, as these types of retailers are used to working with much lower margins than conventional photo shops. This has had a major effect on stand-alone minilabs.

In other countries the growth of in-store processing has been much slower, particularly where serious quality-conscious photographers have a major influence on the market.

In addition to in-store minilabs, there have been, from quite early days, a number of franchise chains for stand-alone minilabs. Like many other franchises, they have had their ups and downs, particularly in a rapidly changing market, where some have found it difficult to stay competitive. The challenge has been to offer the franchisee sufficient support and assistance at an affordable cost and that has not always happened.

The advent of digital photography has had a very marked effect on minilabs, so let us examine this phenomenon. It would in fact be more useful to consider electronic imaging, of which digital photography is only one example.

1 George Scott ex Pako VP
2 UK Government RPI statistics
3 www.konica.jp

CHAPTER 5

The Digital Age

We rarely see much mention of photography these days; the "in thing" is digital imaging. It has had, and is having, a dramatic effect on the photofinishing industry as we have described it. But what is it?

Since 1841, we have been able to produce more or less permanent images of events using a variety of chemical processes and this is called photography, or more recently analogue photography. Similarly, since early on in the 20th century, we have been able to capture and display images of events by various electrical methods. The events are usually captured by sensors, which convert light into electrical signals. These can then be transmitted by wire or radio and converted back to images, which are a close replica of the original event. The best known examples are fax and TV. In the case of fax, the end result is usually an image printed on a piece of paper. However, it can just as easily be displayed on a computer or television screen. In the case of TV, because the images normally include movement, they are produced at a rate of 25 or 30 per second and it is really essential to display them on a screen. However, it is also quite feasible to print any one of these images on a piece of paper. The ability to store the electrical signals so as to view them at another time came considerably later.

During the 1960s and 1970s, several types of electronic sensors had been used to transmit images from spacecraft. Some people in the printing industry, producing plates, were also using electronic scanners to make separation negatives from transparencies, but there was nothing that affected amateur photography and photofinishing in particular. However, a number of things have happened since then to change this.

The first of these was the advent of solid-state image sensors. There are several types, but they all do essentially the same thing. They consist of a large number of very small sensors, arranged in a rectangle, a few millimetres long and wide, which can each produce an electrical signal, proportional to the amount of light falling on it. If we mount one of these image sensors behind a camera lens, in the place normally occupied by the film, we can capture an image electrically by opening the shutter for a short period of time.

The next event was the development of electronic memories for computers. Known as digital memories, they can store large amounts of data in digital form. There are different types of computer memories, including silicon chips, magnetic discs or tapes, CDs and DVDs, but they all essentially serve the same function.

If we combine a solid-state sensor mounted in a camera, and some electronics to read or measure the signals produced by the sensors and then convert these to electrical pulses representing numbers and a computer memory, we have made a digital camera. In the 1960s NASA, Kodak and probably some other organisations had experimented with this type of device but, apart from some exotic space research, they were not of much practical use.

The Sony Mavica

On 25th August 1981, Sony stunned the photographic world by announcing the Mavica, [1] the first electronic camera to have a commercial future. It was a camera similar in size to a single lens reflex. By today's standards it was fairly rudimentary, but it could capture and store colour and black and white images on a floppy disc, which could be displayed on a TV set. The image having been captured as electrical signals, could instantly be transmitted to any part of the world. Sony also announced that they were working on a printer. The Mavica used TV technology and stored the images in an analogue format, different from the way in which later cameras store images.

The camera received mixed reactions; thrill and amazement by some, but shrugged off as of little consequence by others. While It had obvious applications for newspapers, although this had to wait some years, there was not a queue of people waiting to buy one.

Although the announcement was sensational, at the time, many people in the photographic industry took the view that it was not a very important discovery. The quality was not particularly good and the camera was extremely expensive. Most people thought it might have some press applications, but little else. However, other sources, as quoted by the Japan Colour Finishing Association, took it more seriously. Some thought it might affect business in 3-5 years, while others predicted that a major part of the film business would disappear by 1990. [2] These changes in fact took a considerably longer time to materialise.

A very important point for the industry was that the Mavica was produced by an electronics company, which had not previously been associated with photography. It was not too many years later that the established photographic companies, with their enormous investment in research and manufacture of films and papers, were having to face up to losing part of their share of the imaging industry to electronics companies.

During the next decade a number of companies including Kodak, Fuji, Canon, Nikon, Casio, Sony, Hewlett Packard and Epson, introduced a variety of models, most of which used digital storage, so that by the early 1990s it was apparent that digital cameras were here to stay. Gradually companies like Kodak began to use the word "imaging" rather than "photography" to embrace both electronic and conventional picture taking. None of these cameras had much effect on the photofinishing industry, which continued to grow as the sales of colour films increased until just before the Millennium.

Camcorders

The first example of electronic imaging to affect the photofinishing industry was the emergence, at the end of the 1970s, of very small video cameras, which used solid-state sensors, combined with compact video recorders to produce what are now called camcorders. Several manufacturers, principally Sony, Canon and JVC, were working on such devices and the manufacturers of amateur 8mm cine cameras assumed that their products would soon become obsolete. Despite the fact that amateur camcorders were still several years away, most manufacturers stopped production of 8mm cine film cameras almost immediately. This started a run down of amateur cine processing. Although the services are still available 25 years later, they are mainly used by professionals working for television.

Until the late 1990s, there was not much connection between digital photography and photofinishing. Compared with pictures taken on film, nowadays often called analogue photography, digital photography was much less significant in numbers. Furthermore, the amateur photofinishing industry did not have any equipment or technology to make prints from digital images, the only readily available method was to use a computer printer.

The first serious moves to use electronic, specifically digital, techniques were made by professional photographers. Once an image has been captured in digital form then a number of options, not available or very difficult with film, become possible. Modifying or combining several pictures, as is commonly done in advertising, is much simpler and, in addition, digital images can be transmitted over telephone lines or by radio link.

In the early 1990s, with the exception of possibly a few press photographers, professionals did not use digital cameras, and so the digital images were produced by scanning negatives or transparencies. A scanner shines a narrow beam of light onto the film and the beam is moved so as to scan the whole of the image. A sensor on the other side of the film measures the amount of light transmitted and after digitising, this is stored in the computer. In the case of colour, scanning is done through blue, green and red filters. The arrangement of the light and sensor varies considerably. Some scanners use a narrow beam of light deflected by a mirror, while others move the film relative to the light and still others use a large light source and a number of small sensors. Some scanners use three coloured lights, while others use sensors with colour filters. Scanners vary considerably in their resolution depending on the requirements for the eventual use of the images. Print scanners are widely used, but here the density of the image is measured by reflection. When the highest quality is required, it is usual to scan the original camera film.

Kodak Photo CD

Once the idea of images in digital form became widespread, it was important to adopt standards for the way in which the information was stored. The industry adopted a number of standards, the most common being TIFF and JPEG, but there are many others. Image files, depending on the resolution, can be quite large varying between, say, 20KB* to several hundred MB* for the highest quality. Storing these on a computer can be a problem as most machines do not have infinite capacity and it is always desirable to have a back-up. During the late 1980s recordable CD technology was developed and in 1990 Kodak launched its Photo CDs.

There was considerable confusion inside Kodak about the potential use of CDs and this did not help in getting the system established. The top management, who were very much mesmerised by the amateur film business, saw this as a method of entering the digital age for snap-shooters, while the people who had developed the product, believed it to be more suited for the professional market and this, in fact, proved to be correct.

Kodak provided the scanner, the recorder and recordable CDs, and supplied the software for viewing and handling the images on a personal computer. Each CD could hold the scans from up to 100 frames in six different resolutions. These varied from 128 x 192 pixels, suitable for thumbnail prints, to a maximum of 4096 x 6144 pixels, which even by today's standards is a high resolution. The photographer could have some images scanned and stored on the CD and at a later date could add further images until the disc was full. The system achieved only moderate success probably because at first there was only limited demand and by 2000, when demand had increased considerably, there were a variety of scanners as well as CD recorders and software which were produced by a number of other manufacturers.

** KB = Kilo Bytes = thousands of Bytes MB = Mega Bytes = millions of Bytes, which is a measure of the size, i.e., the number of digits stored in a file.*

In 1994, Seattle Photoworks, an innovative mail order photofinisher, introduced its "Picture on a Disc" service. They scanned customers' films after processing and saved the images on a floppy disc. The floppies were returned with the films and prints, together with software for viewing and simple image manipulation, on a PC. Due to the limited capacity of a floppy disc, the scans were of relatively low resolution, but adequate for e-mailing and making small prints. It was probably the first of a number of such systems for "computer savvy" amateurs. Photoworks, in addition to offering the service, licensed the system to Spector in Europe. In 1998 Photoworks launched their "Picture on a CD" service, which offered higher resolution scans, together with the viewing software on the CD.

Soon after Seattle Photoworks, Kodak launched a similar system, its "Picture CD" an altogether simpler and lower cost system than the Photo CD. It was intended for the amateur photographer, with photofinishers providing the service, and scanning the colour negative film after processing. The photos were saved on a CD in JPEG format at a resolution of 1024 x 1536 pixels, sufficient for a reasonably sized print. The files were suitable for e-mailing or printing on a home computer. Most photofinishers now provide a similar service, using software and equipment from several other manufacturers.

Following the availability of digital images, a number of companies offered the software to manipulate these images. They vary from relatively simple programs for cropping and making simple enhancements, to elaborate programs such as Adobe Photoshop which makes it possible to effect almost any conceivable alteration to a picture. Photoshop was launched in 1990 and by 2003 had gone through eight versions. It was also issued in various simplified versions for those with more limited aims.

During the 1990s there was considerable convergence between the photographic and graphic arts industries. Graphic artists used much of the same technology, such as photographic negatives as an intermediate for making printing plates, but they had always tried to keep their industry separate. With images for printing now available in digital form and often requiring the same software to manipulate them as is used by the photographic industry, the distinction between them has been somewhat eroded.

Film Writers

Once it became commonplace to manipulate photographic images in digital form, the professional labs were left with the problem of how to print them. At first the method adopted was to convert them back to a negative using a filmwriter. This was a device, bearing some similarity to the laser printers used in most offices, although in practice they were rather more complicated and expensive. Film writers are not new; during the 1970s the Photo Electronics Corporation of West Palm Beach,

Florida, was using one of their own design to produce negatives from Kodachrome transparencies. The routine of scanning, correcting and making a negative, using normal Kodacolor film, gave much better results than optically exposing the very expensive internegative film, which was the method used by most labs at the time.

By the mid 1990s several companies including Agfa, Durst and Kodak had produced printers which could expose colour paper directly from a digital file, cutting out the need for a negative. Some, like the Durst Lambda, which can make prints up to 50" (127 cm) wide by any length, use three lasers to expose the papers, while others use LEDs. These printers became very popular and by 2003 a large proportion of professional prints were made in this way. As we shall see, amateur photofinishers were due to follow a few years later.

Perhaps the first time that photofinishers were forced to enter the world of digital imaging was in 1996 when the APS (Advanced Photo System) was introduced. The consortium, which introduced the system, stipulated that every photofinisher who processed the films had, amongst other things, to include an index print with each processed film. This is a print consisting of thumbnail images of each negative. To produce these by optical printing is not practical, so the method adopted was to make a low-resolution scan of each of the negatives and then to make a composite print from these.

This presented quite a challenge, high-speed printers such as the Agfa MSP run at 20,000 frames an hour, i.e., taking less than one-fifth of a second each. Most film scanners at that time took several seconds per frame. A number of companies including Kodak, Agfa and Gretag produced high-speed scanners suitable for this purpose. In addition, the computers controlling these scanners had to format the scans so as to make up to 20 of them onto a 4" x 6 " print. Kodak, Gretag and Agfa produced digital printers, which were able to expose these onto regular photo paper. After processing, the index prints had to be "mated up" with the normal prints, quite a considerable task.

Printing Digital Images

By the late 1990s digital cameras, having improved in performance and dropped in price, were beginning to sell to amateurs in increasing numbers and sales of conventional films had peaked. The only practical way for snap-shooters to print images from digital cameras was by using an inkjet printer connected to a home PC. In theory, it would have been possible to use the printers used by wholesale photofinishers to produce index prints, but this was not really practical. Apart from cost, there was also the problem of how to get the files, which had been saved in the camera memory chips, to the labs.

This began to change after 1998 when Fuji, amongst others, launched digital minilabs which could produce prints on normal silver halide photographic paper from images, such as those produced by digital cameras, or scanned from films or prints.

Digital, as opposed to analogue, minilabs do not project an image of a negative onto the photographic paper. Instead, they shine light which is generated from the electronic signals produced by the scanner or camera. There are several systems, each with slightly different characteristics.

The most advanced systems used by Fuji, Konica, Agfa, Noritsu and others, exposes the paper using three lasers controlled by the picture signals. A variant of this uses LEDs instead of lasers.

Another system uses a digital light valve, which consists of several million minute mirrors etched onto a silicon chip. The image signals are used to move these mirrors a tiny amount, so as to deflect light from a powerful projection lamp on to or away from the paper.

A third system uses what is in fact an electronic negative and one of its main uses is to convert a film or analogue minilab to print digital images. A liquid crystal screen, similar in principle to the LCDs used on laptop computers, is placed in the light path of the printer in the place of a normal film negative. In response to the electronic signals, it forms a large number, (several million), colour filters of varying densities and colours which define the image on the colour paper. It offers the owners of older minilabs the chance to convert to digital at considerably lower cost. However, by 2003 they had not become very popular, possibly because exposing the paper is only one of the requisites of a digital minilab. A digital minilab also requires a large amount of software, which probably does not exist for digital negative carriers and very few companies are in a position to provide this.

There have been attempts to produce digital minilabs using printing materials other than silver halide. Kodak and HP formed a partnership under the name Phogenix to produce minilabs based on Inkjet printing. The idea was to produce much lower cost equipment, not requiring chemicals, which was suitable for locations with relatively low volumes. The venture was aimed at small retail shops and possibly hotels and convention centres who wanted to provide an in-house printing service. In early 2003, just as the labs were due to be launched, the partners decided to abandon the project. Whether it was a conflict of interest between Kodak and HP, or the economics were not right, has never been made clear.

Also in 2003, Noritsu, in conjunction with Epson, launched a small output minilab which also used inkjet printing, presumably aimed at a similar part of the market as Phogenix. It is almost certainly a niche market, relying on speed and possibly convenience, and selling premium products such as enlargements and calendars, if only because the cost of the ink jet materials is considerably higher than Silver Halide paper. Other products closely related to this include the Epson Gemini printer specifically intended for social photographers.

Digital minilabs have a number of advantages compared with the analogue models which, by mid 2003 were no longer offered for sale in the US and Europe. In combination with a scanner, they can handle all types of images, whatever their origin, be that colour, black and white, negative or transparency film, prints or digital files. Using ever more sophisticated software, it is much simpler to cope with different sizes of originals, and print sizes, without having to change negative carriers, lenses or the printing paper. Most important, the latest digital printers are able to measure and correct images in a much better way than analogue minilabs, which are printing from negatives, resulting in superior quality without operator intervention and therefore substantially fewer rejects. For example, the software can correct for underexposed shadows, overexposed highlights, remove dust marks and correct for red-eye. As a consequence, one machine with a few accessories, can now produce, not only the work traditionally offered by photofinishers, but also much of that available from professional labs.

Most of the large wholesale photofinishers have used minilabs for many years. Initially they were installed for reprinting rejects and handling reprint orders and, for at least a year after the Advanced Photo System was launched in 1996, they were the only method available for printing APS films. Up to 2003, the majority of digital images were printed using minilab equipment as there were very few labs which had installed high-speed digital printers with outputs approaching 20,000 prints per hour, the standard for analogue photofinishing printers.

Kodak produced their I lab, a digital printer with an output of 5,000 – 7,000 prints per hour, but by the end of 2003 it appeared to be in use only in Kodak photofinishing labs.

Gretag had designed both high-speed scanners and the Cyra digital printer but all work stopped when the company went into receivership in 2002. In 2003, KIS Photo-Me took over this division of Gretag and restarted production of Cyra printers. A number of them were installed by the end of 2003. Initially their output was about 10,000 prints per hour but this was doubled in 2004. This printer has proved to be very reliable and by 2005 more than 100 had been installed.

Agfa were also working on a high-speed digital printer and deliveries began during the course of 2004. By the following year it was in use in several labs, but they had their work cut out to catch up with the Cyra printers.

Changing to digital printing has similar benefits for photofinishers to those enjoyed by digital minilabs. However, it may be a number of years before the process becomes widespread. In the first instance the printers and the computer systems required to control them are still at an early stage of development and, in addition, the investment required in order to convert to digital working is enormous.

Some idea of the scale of the task can be gained by considering the amount of data to be handled. To keep the 20,000 prints per hour printers running, an image has to be fed to the printers every one-sixth of a second. Bearing in mind that most of the files are at least 1 MB and possibly much larger, the lab requires very powerful servers and large local storage. A lab using high-speed digital printers and making the image corrections carried out by most digital minilabs, has to achieve this in one- tenth of the time or less.

The volume of wholesale photofinishing is declining with the drop in film sales and with prices driven down by the large retailers, the investment required to convert to total digital printing is beyond the reach of many labs.

We are now in the unusual situation that a relatively small minilab is as advanced in its technology as is the largest photofinisher. A minilab can produce equal or better quality and a bigger variety of products, faster than a large photofinisher. For the bulk of standard prints produced from 35mm colour negative film, the large photofinisher still has a cost advantage, but this is partially offset by the collection and delivery costs.

The challenge for the wholesale labs is to reduce their costs for prints from digital files, so as to compete with minilabs on price and quality. How this works out in the future, will no doubt affect the relative positions of retail and wholesale photofinishing.

The emergence of digital minilabs has greatly expanded the number of minilabs in supermarkets, drug store chains and similar retailers and has consequently changed the role of free-standing minilabs. With a few exceptions, in certain locations with very large traffic, it is no longer practical for a free-standing minilab to rely entirely on work from amateurs. Most of the successful businesses now do some work for professional photographers and this, in turn, has affected professional labs amongst whom there have been many mergers to form fewer, but larger, businesses.

On-line Photofinishing

A further development of photofinishing, which began in 1999, is a result of the spread of internet usage. There are now an increasing number of labs, which will accept digital images sent via the internet. The so-called "on-line labs" will store these images in albums and produce prints, usually within 24 hours or less. Some are quite large specialist companies delivering by post, while others are operated either by wholesale photofinishers or high street minilabs. In effect, they are the modern equivalent of mail order with the obvious convenience for the user, of not having to go to the mail box. As of 2006 there were a few specialist labs, some making 1,500,000 or more prints on a busy day, but the majority were much smaller. As survivors of the "dot com bubble", a few were becoming profitable, but for the majority it was still a case of investing for the future.

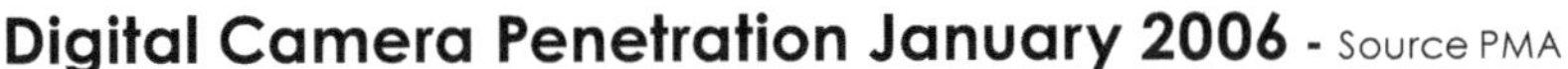

Digital Camera Penetration January 2006 - Source PMA

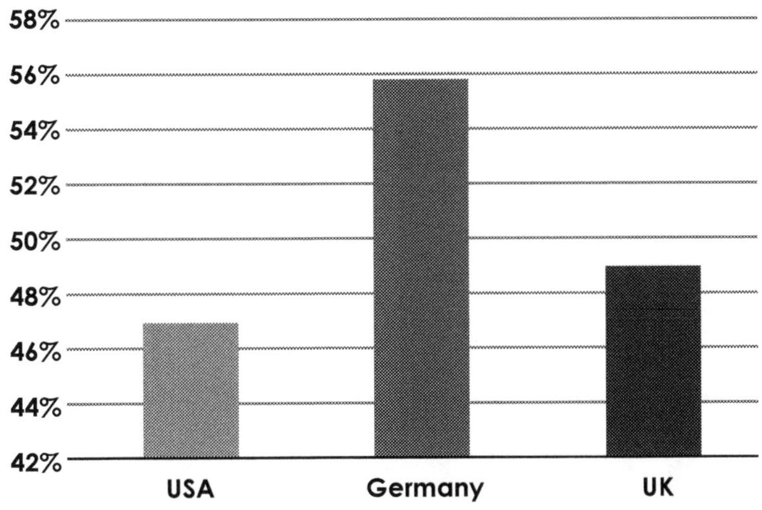

The success of the on-line labs is closely tied up with their ability to promote their services and the ease of use of their websites. The whole of the photofinishing industry is faced with the challenge of getting the snap-shooters to print at least a proportion of their digital images and also in getting over the message of the advantage of obtaining these from a lab rather than producing them at home. This is at a time when a considerable proportion of the digital cameras are sold by electronics stores, on-line or otherwise, and these are also busy selling home computer printers, paper and ink cartridges. To add to the difficulties, DVD players, connected to TV sets, have become much more widespread and many of these players and many home computers have software for putting on slide shows from images saved on CDs. This is making the viewing of holiday and family snaps on the family TV a social occasion and reduces the demand for prints.

Digital labs, both on-line and via retail shops, have increased their offerings and, in addition to prints, supply a wide range of other products such as greeting cards, calendars, photo albums, T shirts and mugs. While it has been possible to produce these from film, the ability to add personal messages has made them much more attractive. Some companies, such as Shutterfly in San Francisco, who by the end of 2003 were one of the leaders of the on-line labs, were printing cards, calendars and photo books using Indigo digital printers, a process very similar in result to offset litho, except that they do not require printing plates and hence each print can be different.

By 2005, the competition between labs producing prints from digital cameras had become fierce and prices of prints, particularly the 4"x 6" (10 x 15 cm) size, were dropping very quickly and the move to other products such as calendars and albums has accelerated.

Film Camera and Digital Camera per 1000 Person - Source PMA

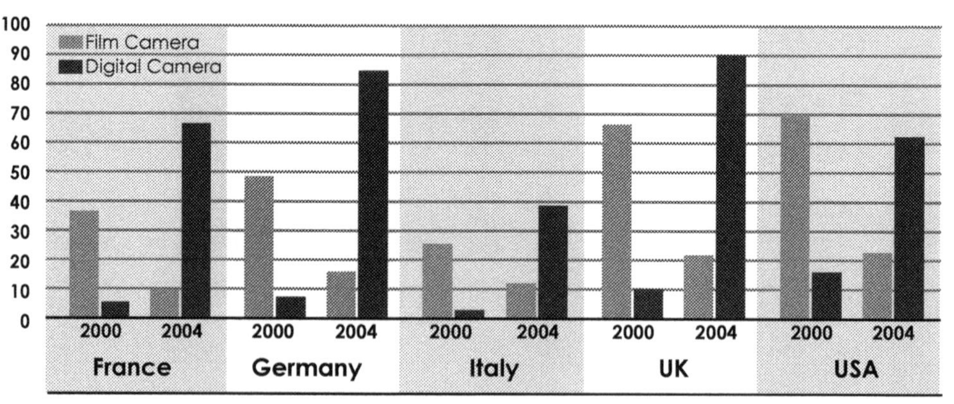

A big challenge for photofinishers and retailers has been to encourage amateur photographers to bring their images for printing by making it as simple as possible.

Many retailers have installed kiosks into which all kinds of digital images can be downloaded from cameras, storage cards, CDs or camera phones. They are connected either to a minilab or to a remote wholesale photofinisher. Some are self- service, where the customer can view his images and select those they wish to order, others are operated by the shop or minilab staff. In addition to accepting images for printing, many can also produce CDs for archiving or viewing or printing on a home PC. Frequently ,the kiosks include a printer, especially in locations where there is no minilab.

Camera Phones

A new phenomenon became apparent in 2005. For years, the photofinishing industry has been using the phrase "carry a camera" in advertising, in an attempt to increase picture taking. Suddenly camera phones emerged and sales of these now exceed ordinary cameras. Before long a large proportion of the population will always be carrying a camera and be taking far more images than anybody had ever imagined. The effect that this has on photofinishing will no doubt change over the coming years.

Digital photography differs from conventional photography in that many more images are exposed, but a much smaller proportion are printed. There are several printing options and different types of photofinishers have a challenge to obtain their share. There are lots of predictions, which no doubt will only be realised with hindsight, as to which numbers of digital images will be printed on a home PC, or by the photofinishing industry, stored as CDs for viewing on a PC or TV set, or sent to friends and relatives as e-mails. The future for photofinishers is both exciting and challenging. What seems certain is that the industry will go through many more changes in the next quarter century, if not before.

1 Sony Corporation Press Release 24th Aug 1981 see www.digicamhistory.com/1980_1983.htmlom/1980_1983.html
2 JCFA History of Japanese Photofinishing 2002, Page 33

CHAPTER 6

The USA

It is not surprising that the United States is the largest photofinishing market, but whether that will still be true by the middle of the 21st century is open to conjecture.

It all started in Rochester in 1888 when George Eastman introduced the "Kodak", the first inexpensive camera, with the slogan "You push the button - we do the rest" . The $25 camera contained enough film for 100 exposures and, after the pictures had been taken, it was sent back to Kodak in Rochester with $10, where it was reloaded with fresh film and returned to the customer, together with a set of prints.

The Trade Association

What really got the snap-shooter going, and also the developing and printing industry, was the launch in 1900 of the first Brownie camera which cost $1 plus 15 cents for the film. There was no longer any need to send the cameras or films back to Kodak because photo shops, photographers and some pharmacies, who were selling processing chemicals to amateurs, started developing and printing the films themselves. Many of the shops soon had more films than they could process and set up separate businesses for this part of the work. These processing businesses worked only for shops and hence were styled wholesale photofinishers.

George Eastman's success in marketing his inexpensive cameras and films resulted in a rapid growth of the industry. In 1924 the Photo Finishers Association of America, whose aim was to promote the growth of the industry, was founded in Iowa with 273 members. Only one year later it had grown to 1000 members.

From early on the association held an annual convention and it was at the 1927 convention that Kodak published some statistics. In 1926 they listed 6,200 photo finishers only 2,000 of whom were full-time finishers, the remainder being studios and commercial photographers who also did some photofinishing. During that year 70% of all cameras cost less than $5 at retail prices and 85% of them cost less than $10. This was a good indication of Kodak's aim in making photography a popular pastime.

In the early years, the seasonal nature of the business was a serious problem because most of the work was concentrated in a few weeks of the summer with virtually no work in winter. The association's magazine records many attempts to find work for the winter months. As early as 1925 there were articles suggesting that finishers should actively promote photo greeting cards and many of the smaller finishers also owned portrait studios.

A big breakthrough in extending the season came in 1931 with the invention of flash bulbs. GE produced more than 1 million in the first year and this dramatically reduced the winter slump.

Arthur Cunningham, a finisher in Uttica, New York, one of the activists of the association who had been president in 1929, claimed that the depression years of the early 1930s had not ravaged the industry. Customers on a lower income, who could no longer afford photography, were replaced by more affluent people who, although they might have travelled in the past, were now trading down to more affordable pleasures, such as picture-taking. The association's magazine claimed that, in the first six months of 1930, there had been more growth than in any previous similar period.

In 1934, R.J Wilkinson, a finisher from Jackson, Michigan, became executive manager of the association, a post he held until his retirement in 1967. Wilkie, as he was affectionately known, was a tireless campaigner on behalf of the industry. As the publisher of Photo Developments, the association's magazine, which had since been renamed Photo Marketing, he wrote countless articles and editorials pleading with finishers to produce top quality work and not to get into a spiral of price cutting. Unlike many other countries, in the US it was illegal to fix prices, so In the early years the association published the price lists of some of their members stating that these were fair prices below which it was not possible to do good quality work.

Arthur Cunningham's price list for July 1924 showed a developing charge of $0.15 for six exposure films and $0.25 for 10 -12 exposure films. Prints, depending on size, were $.05, $.06, $.07 each. 4" x 6" enlargements were $0.10, while the larger 5"x7" prints were $0.15. This meant that developing and printing a film usually came to considerably less than $1. This level of pricing was common until after World War 2 and the beginning of colour.

Whether these campaigns to avoid price competition had much effect is not clear although, in April 1936, when there was a suspicion that Shell Petroleum were going to by-pass photo dealers and finishers with special film and print offers at gas stations, he persuaded them that it would not be in their interest to get into photography.

Some of Wilkie's articles, such as the editorial in the June 1935 edition, entitled "WHOSE country is this?", sound rather strange by today's standards. He is telling his members to fight the chain stores that are threatening to import foreign films and set up their own large finishing plants, by-passing local finishers and drug stores. Little could he have guessed what the finishing and retail industry would look like half a century later, not to mention that half of Kodak's business would then be outside the United States.

The industry continued to grow and by 1939, according to a Department of Commerce survey, finishers were doing $16,000,000 of business.[1]

For many years the finishers' trade association had worked very closely with the dealers' trade association both to expand the market and to protect their interests. In 1946 they amalgamated to become the MPDFA, the Master Photo Dealers and Finishers Association. Later on it absorbed a number of other organisations to become the PMAI, Photo Marketing Association International with about 20,000 members, half of them outside the United States.

Many of the early photofinishers built some of their own equipment but by the 1930s most were using either Kodak or Pako machinery, although a number of other manufacturers had also built contact printers and processors.

As early as 1925, silver had become an issue, but not for environmental reasons; this was to happen much later. US manufacturers of films and paper had become the world's largest user of silver bullion. Eastman Kodak were using 3½ tons of pure silver per week, which meant that, during the week of 18th April 1925, when the price was $0.537 per ounce, they must have spent over $60,000 on the metal. In those days $3,000,000 per annum was a considerable sum and Kodak suggested to finishers that they could recover some of this silver from fixing baths. Photo Developments published articles telling finishers how they could do this.

High summer temperatures, particularly in the Southern States, were a problem especially where cool water was not available. In 1925, one article under the heading "Ultra Modern Temperature Control", described how a finisher had adapted a Kelvinator ice maker for cooling developer tanks from 80°F to 65°F (27°C - 18°C). Fifty years later this was much less of a problem, as films and paper were by then processed at very much higher temperatures.

Kodak produced the vast majority of films and paper, with Agfa, Ansco, Haloid and Dupont supplying only a small amount.

Contrary to the situation in Europe, there were very few 35 mm films, the market being dominated by low-cost Kodak roll-film cameras. These initially used 116 and

120 sized films which produced acceptable contact prints up to 2 1/4" x 3 1/4" but, later, as the quality of films and inexpensive cameras improved, the smaller 127 film size, from which the finishers produced enlargements to 3 1/4" x 4 1/2", became very popular.

Deckled-edge prints were fashionable for a number of years. Print curling was a perennial problem for finishers and a number of companies were offering various pieces of equipment to straighten the prints. Closely related to this problem was that posed by glossy prints, which had a tendency to stick on glazing drums and were a source of trouble for finishers for many years. Over the years the paper manufacturers gradually eliminated these problems.

Kodak introduced home movie cameras in 1923, initially using black and white films, but followed by Kodachrome in 1935. The black and white films were processed by Kodak and a number of other finishers, but Kodachrome was sold as "process paid" and had to be sent back to Kodak.

The Beginning of Colour

In 1936 Kodachrome 35mm film was launched and this was the serious beginning of still colour photography for the amateur. Kodak, probably with some justification, considered that the process was too complicated and difficult for photofinishers and sold the film as "process paid" complete with a mailing envelope to return the film to their lab in Rochester. This was followed in 1942 by Kodacolor colour negative film and again Kodak decided to keep the processing in-house, but allowed photo dealers to handle it.

At that time, the fact that Kodak kept the colour processing to itself was not too serious a problem as photographic materials were in short supply during the war and many photofinishers were, in any case, working for the government. Photography as a hobby took a little time to get going after the war, until film was again freely available. This lasted for a short while but, by 1949, it was estimated that there were 34 million still cameras[2] and over 1 million 8 and 16 mm cine cameras in use in the United States.[3]

The vast majority of photography was still black and white, mostly using Kodak, but with also a few Ansco and Agfa films. The sale of Kodacolor and Kodachrome films grew very quickly and Kodak opened several processing labs in various parts of the US. They offered a print service for both materials, the latter on an opaque white plastic film base.

Pavelle Color

Prior to the Kodacolor colour print service which was carried out by Kodak in Rochester, no amateur colour print service had existed. Ansco decided not to set up their own processing service and in 1946, Leo and Si Pavelle, who had been custom B&W photofinishers, supplying professionals and advanced amateurs in New York since 1936, set up Pavelle Color in order to produce colour prints from transparencies using Ansco Printon. Printon was based on Agfa transparency film, but was made on an opaque white film base.

Pavelle Color was the first independent, highly automated, colour lab in the US. There was no suitable equipment available at the time, so they designed and built their own printers and processing machines. At its peak, Pavelle Color had 12 printers, no doubt working long hours during the busy season.

The Pavelle processors were enormous twin-track machines running at 20 ft per minute and producing close on 6,000 prints per hour.

Printing colour transparencies onto a reversal print material is, in theory, a little simpler than printing colour negatives. Provided that everything stays under control, which was no small feat in the late forties, the print should be identical to the transparency. Corrections could be made visually, which is much easier than with negatives. In the case of the Pavelle printers, the transparencies were pre-coded prior to printing. Printing was from mounted transparencies, which were placed into a carrier which swung out from the printing position to make loading easier. They were nicknamed "titty printers" because of the hazard of the swinging film carriers to the, mainly female, operators.

The lab started with 50 staff, a number which later grew to several hundred. Initially operating in New York City, a collection and delivery service to camera stores was provided three times each day. In 1951 the service was extended nationally providing a turn-round of a few days. The main competitor was Kodak, who offered a similar service, but took about two weeks to deliver the prints.

An idea of the problems which the Pavelle brothers had to solve is given in the talk that Leo Pavelle and Lloyd Varden gave to the Photographic Society of America about their 10 years experience of colour processing. [4]

Due to the considerable exposure latitude of black and white films, it had long been the norm to ignore the manufacturer's processing instructions. It came as quite a shock when the instructions for colour, which were much more complicated, could no longer be ignored. Many of the steps were critical and had to be adhered to closely.

To make things worse, there was no experience in operating the machinery which they had designed and they had to overcome many quite serious problems. Examples they gave included chemical deposits in the processor tanks, causing the rollers of the processing machines to seize up. This took considerable time and effort to solve. Handling colour chemistry on the scale of their lab presented a number of further challenges which, at that time, only Kodak had had to deal with. Additional problems, which took many years to overcome, were the variations between batches of films and printing materials and their changes depending on storage conditions. The effect of these problems was that they had to remake sometimes as much as 50% of the work and, at best, never less than 25%. This was something that black and white finishers had never anticipated.

In 1956 the business was sold to Technicolor who wanted to expand into photofinishing as an extension to their cinema-processing activities. However, they soon found that there was not much connection and their involvement did not last for very long.

Some years after Pavelle Color was founded, Drewry Color in Los Angeles provided a similar service, although probably on a much smaller scale.

Anti–trust Proceedings

By the early 1950s, when colour photography was starting to become popular, many photofinishers were concerned that Kodak's practice of tying together its film and photofinishing services would eventually deprive them of their business. At that time Kodak colour film, sold by Kodak inclusive of the price of photofinishing, accounted for about 90% of the US colour film market. The Government took out anti-trust proceedings and as a result, in 1954, Kodak entered into a consent decree. This required Kodak to stop including the price of photofinishing with its films and to supply the equipment, materials and know-how to any photofinisher who wished to process colour films.

Kodak then released both the Kodacolor colour print and the Kodachrome transparency process. They had always claimed, possibly with some justification, that the colour processes were beyond the ability and resources of photofinishers. Not only did colour processing require much more sophisticated equipment than for black and white, but chemists and trained quality-control staff were essential in order to provide an acceptable service.

Kodak's photofinishing operation in Rochester and elsewhere were on a far larger scale than the cottage industry type of operations of the hundreds of independent photofinishers. All the chemistry was mixed on site from raw materials under the supervision of chemists as no one had any experience of preparing packs of chemicals which could be mixed without the facilities and staff of a chemical manufacturing plant.

Chemicals for processing colour films and prints consist of dozens of constituents which have to be mixed in exact proportions and in a certain sequence. Once mixed, they have a very short shelf-life. If one attempts to simplify the operation by weighing out the constituents for a certain size of mix, they have to be stored separately until they are ready to be mixed. To make matters worse, some of the chemicals require the addition of preservatives if they are to be stored for any length of time. This was beyond the capability of most photofinishers, so Kodak produced packs of chemicals for the Kodacolor negative film and print processes which were reasonably easy to mix. The Kodachrome process, however, was so complicated that for the next 40 years Kodak only published the formulae and left the photofinishers to struggle as best they could.

For Kodacolor, the other material was colour paper. This had a limited shelf-life and needed to be kept cool, both in transport and storage. Just to make life more difficult, there were considerable variations in sensitivity between batches and this changed further during storage and also between the time when the paper was exposed and processed. Over the years, as a result of intense competition, mainly from Fuji, the quality of colour paper has improved dramatically and most of these problems have now been resolved.

The most important piece of equipment required for printing colour negative films was an efficient colour printer. Kodak decided that model 1599, which they used in Rochester, was far too complicated and expensive for the independent photofinishers.

They adapted a black and white printer, which was then in widespread use and this became the Eastman Kodak model IVC, the first colour printer sold to independent photofinishers. It made three successive exposures through blue, green and red filters each controlled by a photocell. By today's standards it was a crude piece of equipment, but it worked extremely well. Perhaps it is in a similar relationship to the Ford model T, compared with today's near-perfect cars.

Kodak did not manufacture film processors, but there were a number of manufacturers, including Pako, whose B&W "dip and dunk" processors could easily be adapted to process Kodacolor colour negative films. Kodak did, however, supply processors for rolls of colour paper. Pako quickly introduced colour versions of their roll-paper processors and, within a few years, introduced their own colour printers.

In addition to Kodak and Pako, a number of other companies who had manufactured black and white finishing machinery, produced colour printing and processing equipment. Names such as the Plasto Foto Corporation of New York, Fotopak of New Jersey, Dakota of Los Angeles and Dean Specialty Works of San Antonio Texas have long since disappeared, although some may have become part of other companies. Companies such as Hills and Houston Fearless survived for much longer, although their main business may no longer be in the photographic industry.

The processing of Kodachrome was extremely difficult as it required very critical chemical controls. A number of US photofinishers set up for this by using processing machines designed for the cine industry. The results were somewhat mixed and some finishers privately admitted that they could not match Kodak's quality. Many had difficulty in getting sufficient work and dropped their prices to half or less than those of Kodak. Several of them quite quickly discontinued processing Kodachrome. Within a few years there were hardly any independent photofinishers still doing so.

Pavelle Color, who were one of the first to take up Kodachrome processing, must have had their share of problems, some of which they believed were not of their own making. They sued Kodak for not giving them enough technical assistance to handle such a complicated process and Kodak, wanting to avoid the adverse publicity of such a case, settled for a substantial sum the day before the court hearing.

An interesting sideline to this concerns William J Brown,[5] a very talented photographic engineer, who had a number of businesses in Rochester. In the early 1950s he had been building black and white film processing machines under the Kryptar brand and also had at various times been coating black and white films. After the consent decree he was one of the first to take a licence from Kodak to process Kodachrome films. He leased an empty mill building in Brockport N.Y. near Rochester and, using his own machinery, set up a Kodachrome processing facility, calling the company Dynacolor.

As was the case with some other labs, he found that few dealers were willing to send customers' films to an untried processor, leaving him with an underused plant. What changed all this, is reputed to have been related by a Kodak photofinishing salesman in Texas, who found that, shortly after Thanksgiving Day, there was virtually no Kodachrome processing within his area. Apparently, the largest photofinisher in his territory used William Brown's processing machines. However, a high-volume B&W processing machine had broken down and they were unable to fix it. They called Brown, who flew down immediately to repair it. When they asked him how much they owed him, he said it was nothing as it was his machine that had broken down.

The grateful owner said he wanted to do something for Brown, who told him that he had a new Kodachrome plant in Rochester and suggested that he send his work to Brown rather than to Kodak. Within a few days, sacks of films started arriving.

There were other rumours, including one that Brown needed finance to operate and expand his plant and that, when he tried to get finance from a Chicago bank, the deal was mysteriously blocked. No doubt that is the nature of competition! Brown, being a very enterprising man, called all his friends, who in turn called others and they all bought shares in his company. For a time Dynacolor flourished and not so long after, when many of the original patents had run out, they started coating Dynachrome, which was a Kodachrome-type film. In a limited sort of way the film was quite successful and a few years later, when 3M were anxious to expand their photographic business, they bought the Dynacolor company.

What follows from the consent decree in 1954 to the Millennium is an interesting story, for which we are indebted to a number of people, including Donald Becker, who joined the industry after war service and later became chairman of one of the major companies of the photofinishing industry, Fox Photo Inc.

Following the consent decree in 1954, many photofinishers decided to take on colour processing, mostly Kodacolor, using a mixture of Kodak, Pako or home-built equipment. The labs, which were just starting out, had no idea of the economics or pricing involved and so followed Kodak's lead, charging about $5-$5.50 for processing and printing an eight-exposure roll of film. This compared to about $1 for an equivalent black and white film. For a considerable time there were far fewer rolls of colour film, but it soon became apparent that colour was potentially far more profitable, certainly for Kodak, who by then had a considerable volume of work and, more importantly, had mastered the technique.

It was an exciting time for the industry; the Photo Developments magazine had, for several years contained numerous articles about the opportunities of colour processing, estimates of costings and details of techniques as well as speculation on how long black and white photography would continue. As early as February 1943, an editorial had appeared telling photofinishers to start planning for the post-war years, when there was likely to be a practical process for making colour prints on paper. By the end of the 1950s there was a rapid growth of the industry, which very few had been able to predict with any certainty. Eastman Kodak had an enormous R&D department and they were producing films, papers, cameras and finishing equipment in double-quick time. While the consent decree had taken away a share of their photofinishing business, this did not stop it growing rapidly and becoming one of the world's most profitable companies. On the contrary, it probably stirred up the company and stopped it from becoming a sleeping giant or a stumbling elephant, at least not for many years.

Most photofinishers, processing B&W films in the 1950s were fairly small, very few employing more than 50 staff. Output, by today's standards, was very low as prints were often made from cut negatives onto sheet paper. Some of the workers, and most of the printers were female, could make 700-800 prints per hour. In addition, processing cut paper and matching the prints up with the negatives was a very labour-intensive operation.

Explosive Growth

Initially the volume of colour films was very small and the equipment required for colour processing was beyond the reach of many finishers. Finance was not easy to obtain and as a result there were many mergers so that, by the early 1960s, several of the merged companies went public to raise money for expansion, colour processing equipment and further mergers.

One example of this was Fox Photo of San Antonio, Texas, which merged with Stanley Photo of St. Louis, Missouri, in 1961 and then went public. Between 1961 and 1974 the merged company bought up 40 black and white labs to create a network of large labs. Its turnover was about $5 million, which was a considerable sum in those days; it meant that they were probably processing over 1 million rolls of film per annum, a very large number by the standards of that time, since most other labs had turnovers of $1 million or less.

Another group, Colorcraft Corp., was formed in 1960, the result of the merger of three North Carolina finishers, Strawbridge Studios, of Durham, Carolina Photo of Fayetteville and Browning Photo of Wilmington . In 1967 it was acquired by Fuqua Industries, a conglomerate which continued to buy-up other finishers for the next decade or more.

One of the earliest colour processors to go public was Bremson Photo of Kansas City, Missouri which then merged with District Photo, Washington DC and Lyle Briggs of Rockford, Illinois in the late 1950s. Eventually this became District Photo which over the years bought up many mail-order finishers of which it consequently became by far the largest.

Kiosks

A number of changes took place in the way in which customers were served. In the 1960s Fotomat started the marketing concept of kiosks located in parking lots in strip malls. Here snap-shooters could drop off their films and pick up their prints without even getting out of their cars. This was unique to the US, probably due to the much earlier growth of the use of motor cars than in Europe and Japan. The kiosks were located as close as possible to the road, often some distance away from the shops which were served by the parking lots. Initially, Fotomat contracted out the processing, but later set up several labs of its own.

Space for the kiosks could be rented for between $200 and $400 per month and, on average, they collected 50 rolls of film per day. A few were much busier, collecting up to 200 rolls per day. Kiosks typically took 40-50% of the roll price which at that time was in the range of $6-$7.

It did not take long for some of the photofinishers to follow suit and, by the late 1960s, Fox Stanley had its own kiosks. The number peaked at about 1100 kiosks by the late 1970s, when minilabs started to appear, and they were closed by the mid 1980s.

The kiosks era ended due to opposition from retailers in the strip malls, and cities used all sorts of rules to close them including invoking health and safety rules, such as the requirement of work places to have wash rooms. The advent of increased minimum wage rates also reduced their viability.

Consolidation

Ben Berkey founded Berkey Photo in New York in 1933 and it grew rapidly after going into colour in the mid-fifties and going public in 1961. The expansion involved opening or purchasing a large number of plants all over the US and, after rationalisation, the group ended up with nine plants covering most parts of the country. It became the second largest photofinisher in the US after Kodak, by 1969 its sales having reached $53 million.

Ben Berkey was an ambitious man and, in addition to finishing, started various manufacturing and importing businesses. For some years these were successful but things went out of control and some of these activities started making very large losses. In 1985 the finishing business, whose sales were by now around $125 million was sold for $40 million to Fuqua who merged it with Colorcraft based in Durham, N.C. The enlarged Colorcraft had about 40 labs and sales of $280 million, some 15% of the US market, which was slightly more than Kodak had.

This represented a major concentration of the industry but a number of smaller finishers, such as Calev Photolabs in Long Island, carried on independently for many more years.

As the independent wholesale photofinishers grew, Kodak's share of the market declined. Kodak was concerned not only by the loss of their share of the photofinishing market, but also, as Fuji and Konica became more active in the US, by the loss of the colour paper and chemicals market. In the early 1980's Kodak opened a photofinishing subsidiary, Qualis Photofinishing Co. in Boston. This did not infringe the 1954 consent decree, as it was not selling film with prepaid processing. In 1986 Fox Photo was put up for sale and was purchased by Qualis to protect Kodak's share of the paper and chemicals market.

In 1978 Steve Bostic, who had been with Berkey for seven years, having failed to become president of the group, left to run Nimslo who had developed a 3D process which they hoped would take the amateur photo market by storm. This did not happen, so he left and, in 1982, started the American Photo Group by buying a small finisher using some of his own money and borrowing the rest with the assets of the lab as security. He repeated this process a number of times and within five years had built up the lab group to sales of $78 million. He received a number of approaches from people who had unsuccessfully bid for Fox photo and in 1986 ended up selling to Qualis for $78 million. Kodak by that time were willing to buy labs so as to avoid them falling into the hands of Fuji or Konica and so they had a large number of labs all over the US, more than one in several cities.

Another change, which hastened the mergers, was that up to around 1961 most of the retailers had been single outlets. At that time the chains, such as Walmart, Kmart and others, began to grow and this created strong price competition, so that size and low-cost operation became vital for photofinishers.

Qualex

In 1988 Kodak merged its photofinishing labs with those of Colorcraft and a new company Qualex, based in Durham, North Carolina was formed. As a result of the amalgamation, Qualex had 93 wholesale labs, 53 from Kodak and 41 from Colorcraft, including a number of labs acquired by Colorcraft in previous years including Berkey in 1985. In subsequent years Qualex closed some of these labs where there was overlap and opened new labs in areas where it was not represented. Many of these labs were very big, some processing up to 10 million rolls per annum.

Several companies opposed this merger and Phototron of San Bernadino, California, launched an antitrust suit against Kodak and Fuqua Industries. Phototron employed about 1000 people in 10 labs, not only in California, but also in other states, including Texas. Their complaint was that Kodak and Fuqua, their partner to be, were using Kodak's Colorwatch program to drive them out of business or at least to seriously harm them. Colorwatch was a quality control/marketing program for dealers and finishers. The finishers who joined the program, were monitored by Kodak in order to reach a high standard of quality. Retailers were encouraged to use Colorwatch finishers and were rewarded with extra discounts for Kodak merchandise and benefitted from Kodak advertising credits. The catch for finishers was that, to join the Colorwatch program, they had to use Kodak paper and chemicals exclusively. Phototron claimed that Kodak paper and chemicals cost 50% more than they were paying for materials of equivalent quality and, furthermore, as a result of not being a member of the Colorwatch program, they had lost accounts with Kmart, Thrifty Drug Stores, Kroger Co. and Revco Drug Stores.

In 1991 Qualex bought Phototron.

Initially, Kodak only owned 49% of Qualex, but had secured its paper and chemicals market. A short time afterwards, when Fuqua wanted to get out of the finishing business, it became a wholly owned subsidiary of Kodak.

Fuji and Konica

The formation of Qualex did not bode well for other manufacturers of colour paper and chemicals and Fuji started acquiring finishers. By the end of 1993 they combined the 15 labs they had acquired into Fuji TruColor. Fuji continued buying finishers, in particular five very large labs from Walmart and in 1997 combined these and Fuji TruColor to form Fujicolor Processing.

By this time competition between Kodak and Fuji had become very serious and most of the remaining independent labs decided it was time to get out. Konica were not idle either, when Fotomat got into trouble they took over their labs. In 1997 they purchased the Calev labs which were operating in New York, New Jersey and Connecticut, forming a major part of the Konica Quality Photo chain. In August 1998 Bicknell Photo Service of Portland, Maine, joined the group, which now had five plants on the eastern side and three plants on the west coast with total sales of about $100 million.

The Drugstores

In addition to the independent photofinishers, a number of drug store chains and mass marketers had started their own labs. [6] The first must have been Walgreen, who opened their first lab in Chicago in 1919 next to its head office. Mr. Walgreen, the founder, was very keen to be self-contained and in any case there were not too many photofinishers offering their services to other retailers at that time. The May 1939 edition of the Pepper Pod, the Walgreen staff magazine, describes "The Chicago Studio" as their first lab was called.

The studio consisted of four rooms, each, about 8' x 12'. One room was used for developing the films in 50 gallon tanks, another for drying the films, a third for printing and the fourth for fixing, washing and finishing the prints.

Only very few people worked there, but on busy days, when they handled up to 400 films, some of the executives from the head office next door would come to help out with the billing and sorting. In the next 12 years it moved three times to larger premises. At busy times, 20 years later, in 1939, 65 people were working in the studio, handling from 3000 to 6000 films per day. By the late 1930s, Walgreens had also opened studios in Salt Lake City and Miami.

Many years later, between the late 1960s and 1989 they opened or purchased a further four labs in various parts of the country. In the same period, Eckerd Drugs, one of Walgreen's competitors, had opened seven labs to serve its 1,700 stores in the south eastern parts of the US. Similarly, some of the smaller drug chains as well as the giant Walmart Stores opened their own labs.

The industry changed rapidly in the early 1990s with the introduction of the Advanced Photo System (APS) and the growth of minilabs. The retailers were faced with a dilemma. To equip a large wholesale lab to handle APS films required a capital investment of about $1million, while to install minilabs in all their stores required an even larger investment. Most of the retailers decided to get out of the large lab business and sold these to either Qualex, or in the case of Walmart, to Fuji in 1996.

Mail Order

This left the US with three large groups of wholesale photofinishers, a number of mail order labs and a few smaller independents. The largest of the mail order finishers was District Photo, which was still a private company in the early years of the 21st century, and York Photo, part of the Nashua Corporation, but this was later acquired by District Photo. One of the remaining smaller mail order finishers, Mystic Photos in New England, was acquired by District Photo in 2002.

This left only one other mail order finisher. Seattle Film Works was interesting in that it provided its own free film, which was cine film, cut and spooled in 35 mm cassettes. From this film they provided a unique service, a choice of prints or slides from the same film. Cine film is considerably less expensive than regular amateur film, but requires different processing in order to remove the sound track and this discouraged other finishers from processing their "free films". For many years they managed to attract a loyal clientele encouraged by a combination of low price and the versatility of obtaining slides or prints from the same film. In 1994, Seattle Film Works were also one of the first labs to scan films and put these on a floppy disk, so that customers could e-mail their favourite pictures. In 1998 this was followed by a similar, but improved, facility using CDs and in 1999 they added on-line photofinishing. With the intense competition in the market and the cost of all the development work they had done, Seattle ran into financial trouble and in 2000 were reconstituted as Photo Works.

Minilabs and On-site Processing

The advent of the minilabs introduced further changes in that it brought finishing to retailers and threatened to take some of it away from wholesale photofinishers, which further increased the price and service competition. The first minilabs were stand-alone operations, either single businesses or, as in the case of Motofoto, franchises. In the early 1980s the numbers of minilabs were quite small and were charging fairly high prices so that they did not present serious competition to the wholesale photofinishers. This situation changed when some of the drugstore chains installed minilabs. The discount chains were used to operating on small margins and hence were happy to operate minilabs at very much lower prices than traditional outlets. The minilabs had a further advantage in that they helped to keep customers on the premises for a longer period and thus encouraged them to make other purchases.

Kodak had been somewhat restricted in the way it competed in the retail and photofinishing markets by the consent decrees it was forced to accept in 1921 and 1954. In May 1994, despite widespread opposition, they managed to have these rescinded on the basis that circumstances had changed, in particular that they now competed in the international markets where they no longer held an overwhelming market share. This removed most of the restrictions on the growth of Qualex including the placement of minilabs in retail outlets.

Some of the mass merchandisers installed their own minilabs. However, Qualex provided many of their outlets with minilabs on a "pay by the click" basis. Qualex owned the minilabs and they serviced them, supplied them with all the materials and trained their staff. The minilabs were connected via modems and phone lines to Qualex's headquarters in Durham, North Carolina, where the number of prints made by each machine was recorded and billed to the customer. Any films and prints which the on-site minilabs could not process by the end of the day were collected by the nearest Qualex main lab and then processed overnight. By the late 1990s Qualex had installed more than 10,000 on-site processing labs.

The retailers had a very tight grip on the industry and were not shy in playing off Kodak against Fuji. The stakes were very high, as this not only involved the photofinishing business, colour paper and chemicals, but also the sale of films at the photography counters. It is no wonder that very few independent photofinishers survived the onslaught, even Konica was forced to give up the photofinishing business, the labs being purchased by Fuji.

The business has changed further in the first few years of the 21st century. Film usage, and hence processing, peaked in 2001 at close to 1,000 million rolls. Ever since that time it has been decreasing, in part due to the after-effects of 9/11, but also due to the increase in the use of digital cameras. Drug store chains and mass marketers have, to an increasing extent, made the change to digital minilabs, in many cases installing their own machines as their leasing contracts with Qualex and Fuji came to an end.

A good example is Walmart which, by early in the 21st century, accounted for over 25% of US photofinishing. Having sold its five captive labs to Fuji it embarked on a policy of installing minilabs in all their stores. By offering very low prices at acceptable quality, they have attracted more work, putting pressure on their competitors to reduce their prices. They can keep their minilabs busy even in the low season by regulating what they send out to the wholesale labs operated by Fuji.

The situation with other retailers, who were leasing their on-site minilabs from Qualex, was somewhat different. The "by the click" price for prints made on the minilabs was considerably higher than that charged by the Qualex wholesale labs, so doing work in the stores, other than one-hour work at premium prices, was not an option. Just to make the situation worse, most of the on-site labs installed in the 1990s were not equipped to handle work from digital cameras. As a result, as leases for the on-site minilabs have run out, some of the chains, such as Walgreens, have replaced them with their own machines and are thereby putting even greater price pressures on the Qualex main labs.

Up to the end of 2002, prints from digital cameras could only be made by digital minilabs or by using home PCs. Many of the retail outlets are now equipped with digital minilabs so that even fewer films are sent to the wholesale labs.

Qualex and Fuji have closed some of their main labs and those remaining are faced with replacing their digital minilabs with high-speed digital printers, which by the end of 2002 were only just becoming available. It has created a serious predicament in that it involves a considerable investment at a time when the industry is contracting and under enormous price pressures. The investments are necessary in order for the wholesale labs to reduce their costs and it would be a wise person who could predict the share of the US finishing market that the large labs will command in five or ten years' time.

1 Census of Business US Department of Commerce (1939)
2 Stuart K.G and Mansfield F.W: Talk at National Association of Photographic Manufacturers' Meeting, Cleveland, Ohio (Oct. 14, 1948)
3 Eastman Kodak Publicity Release
4 PSA Color Conference, Rochester, N.Y., May 1956
5 Photographic Historical Society Newsletter, September-October 1999
6 Photo Marketing May 2002 "Onward to on site"

CHAPTER 7

The UK

The UK photofinishing industry has a number of similarities to and differences from that of the United States. Perhaps that is not surprising, considering that George Eastman's first venture abroad, was to London. With his slogan "You press the button – we will do the rest" he set up a photofinishing operation in Harrow in the 1890s, which set the pattern. Once daylight-loading cameras became available, there was no need to send them back to Kodak and many of the professional photographers developed and printed films for amateur photographers. As the number of films increased, specialist businesses, working only for retail shops sprang up in various parts of the country. By the late 1920s there were several hundred wholesale photofinishers in England and, in 1929, they formed a trade association, the Wholesale Photo Finishers Association (WPFA).

Early Days

The UK market was very mixed. There were a number of serious amateurs, who were using expensive cameras, mostly of German manufacture, and looking for first-class results. They usually took their films to photographers or specialist dealers to have them processed. However, far greater numbers were more casual in their photography and used inexpensive box cameras like the baby Brownies. These people were not too demanding and took their film to the chemists, who in turn sent it to independent photofinishers. Unfortunately, a few of these photofinishers were not very concerned about quality which did not help to make photography as popular as it might otherwise have been.

Ron Thompson, whose father started his photofinishing business in the East End of London in 1921 and whom he joined in 1937, tells us about how life was for early photofinishers.

At busy times in the 1930s they employed about 50 people, 40 full time plus an extra 10 in the peak season. The maximum number of films processed was 3,000 per day. In those days all films were hand printed with five grades of paper, most of them by contact, using home-built printing frames, with a few being enlarged. The operators became very experienced in judging exposures, since nothing better was available until much later. In 1955 Ron's father bought an Agfa exposing easel, which measured and controlled the exposures for enlargements and this was a considerable step forward, although by that time many labs were changing to printers using roll paper.

The printer passed the exposed paper to the developer who watched it develop under safe light and then moved the print into the stop bath. Another person placed the print into the fix and then into the wash. A third person then placed the prints on the glazer. All prints were hand-trimmed on all four sides. Prints were numbered on the back with pencil so as to be matched up with the films. The whole procedure was very labour intensive.

Most finishers had been using Kodak paper and chemicals but, in the late 1920s, Agfa and Gevaert became very active and helped the finishers by supplying paper at the beginning of the season, but delaying payment until September. Ron's father changed to Agfa, as did many others.

This was part of the reason why Kodak, as a defensive measure to protect their paper and chemicals business, bought a stake in a number of small finishers, forming the "B" companies.

Ron's father bought the first Hepworth "dip and dunk" film processor. This was of all teak construction and about 40ft long. The machine, which did not include a dryer, was installed in a darkroom. Most films were orthochromatic, and could be processed under yellow safelights, but these were extinguished when the small number of panchromatic films were processed.

The machine was destroyed in an air raid during World War 2 and in 1951 Ron's father bought a new processor, with a capacity of 360 films/hour from Carl Hostert. The machine had PVC tanks, a great step forward. Ilford got them to try out their new Phenidone developer, which lasted for a whole season, compared to Metol-Hydrouinone developers, which, had to be changed weekly. From then on, time and temperature processing was introduced.

The 3,000 films, which were processed on the busiest days in the 1930s, represented about 120,000 films per annum, a ratio of 40 x the peak day compared with the 1990s, when the ratio was about 100. Amateurs did not use flash in those days and, for the most part, restricted their photography to outdoors on bright days. The summer season only lasted about six weeks and the rest of the year was very slack. The takings for the whole month of February were barely sufficient to pay one and a half week's wages.

Before the war a 14 year old girl would have been earning about 4 shillings (£0.2) per week plus 6 pence (£0.025) per hour overtime. Top wages were £2 – £3 per week. During the peak period staff worked from 8am until midnight.

There were very few 35 mm films, possibly only 2–3% of the total. Wallace Heaton, an upmarket camera shop in the West end of London, were the 35 mm specialists. The few 35 mm films were processed separately in fine-grain developer.

After the war, many new finishers started up and, although photography was growing in popularity, the Thompsons found it was difficult or even impossible to increase the number of films. However, with mechanisation the numbers of staff dropped dramatically.

In the 1950s the Thompsons started roll printing with an Ilford Synchromat printer and a continuous processor, probably a Trimatic with a large glazing drum. Ron remembers that prints regularly stuck to the drum, a not uncommon occurrence in those days.

A.W. Richardson of Kodak introduced the double film clip to keep dockets with films and this was a big step forward in avoiding mix-ups, which had been dogging the industry since the early days.

During the war, Ron's brother met E.L.G. Hall in a German prisoner of war camp and taught him about D&P. Hall later became head of The Roll Film Company in Wimbledon, South West London, which was one of Kodak's "B" companies, and had originally been started by Captain Barker, one of the pioneers of photofinishing.

During the late 1960s, by which time Thompsons Photo Service were processing colour films, business was fairly profitable 20% net, 55% gross. Wages were about 25% of takings.

Ron's father had a Boots account (see later) for 50 years, which was cancelled in 1971 with 1 week's notice. The Boots business had provided 80% of the total work and so life became very difficult. Ron closed the business in 1980 and worked for the WPFA, (Wholesale Photofinishers Association), by then renamed APL (Association of Photographic Laboratories), until he retired in 1986. A few years later the APL became part of PMA (Photo Marketing Association).

Other large pre-World War 2 finishers, apart from the Kodak "B" companies included:

- Cross of Enfield in North London
- Scott in East London
- Munns Brothers of Birmingham
- Ormskirk Photofinishers – Mr J.J. Entwistle
- Sheffield Photofinishers – Mr E.R. Mottershaw

- Cooper of Bristol
- Alister Inglis in Scotland,
- Tom Glen in Loch Lomond
- Hamilton Tait of Edinburgh

Bill Holmes

Bill Holmes, another stalwart of the UK photofinishing industry, told us about his early days. From his account it is clear how much improvisation with home-built equipment was common, at least among the smaller photofinishers.

After leaving the Royal Air Force in October 1945, he went to work for A.G. Scott & Co. in Silsden, West Yorkshire. This small company was established about 1930 and had continued to do wholesale developing and printing (D & P) during the war years.

Films were developed in ten-gallon vertical tanks. The temperature was controlled by a lead-covered immersion heater which they switched on in the morning and regularly agitated the solution with a wooden stirrer. The heater was switched off as soon as the correct temperature was reached. The ten-gallon tanks were suitable for 120 size films but not quite deep enough for 116,118,122, or 35mm films (which were looped, with a stainless steel oval ring at the bottom of the loop.)

Later Bill converted these tanks to 12 gallon size by building them up using thin bricks and cement and they worked very well with the longer films,

They used Kodak double clips to attach the films to stainless steel rods, three clips to a rod and seven rods per tank. The rods were lowered separately into the developer tank and, after the correct time, the whole batch would be lifted together and moved into the rinse tank and then the fixer.

After washing, the films were hung in a cabinet, which had four rows of oven-type gas jets in the bottom, which had to be lit with a match. A large electric fan in the top of the cabinet was then switched on to draw the warm air over the films which dried the films in about 20 minutes without drying marks, a not infrequent problem with some of the more modern processing machines.

All the chemicals, which consisted of either powders or crystals, were bought in bulk and weighed out using kitchen scales. This was done during quiet periods and the chemicals, sufficient to make two gallons of developer at a time, were stored in paper bags. The fixer used was Hypo, which they made up by filling a 10 gallon tank with water into which they suspended a cloth bag containing the Hypo crystals. This made up a working solution overnight to which they added acetic acid from a large carboy.

After the films were dry, they were cut up into single negatives and put into the wallet with the docket attached and taken to the printing room, Many of the films at that time were celluloid and highly inflammable and when cut up, the surplus trimmings had to be kept in a fireproof metal container, The Factory Inspector always asked to see this container when he made his regular visits. Bill told us he was quite popular on Bonfire Night (5th November) because he would take all their film trimmings to ensure that the lighting of the bonfire was quite spectacular!

As with other finishers most of the work was making contact prints from cut negatives, a very labour-intensive operation.

Due to the scarcity of roll films, immediately after the 1935/45 war, some people bought large quantities of war-surplus aerial film, which was 5" wide and quite thick. These people called at all the photoworks and offered to buy the old spools and backing paper (he thinks for about three old pence – 3d, each). This thick film was then cut into strips and rolled into the re-used backing papers. It curled and was very difficult to handle.

In 1950 Bill Holmes founded Worth Photofinishers in Keighley at a time when changes were taking place in methods of production. They started with Kodak A printers using cut sheets, until they got the Johnson Keene printer which held the negative and paper in a vertical position and automatically stamped a number on the paper before releasing it down a chute into the developer. Later they used Kodak printers, which had automatic exposure control, and used roll paper to make six prints in a single strip, which considerably cut down the developing work and handling.

A series of rubber stamps marked with the number of prints and the price of the order were used for pricing. The top and bottom of the docket were stamped and the bottom part was retained for invoicing at a more convenient time. All their deliveries were made by motorcycle and box sidecar. The service time was 48 hours.

In the early 1950's Worth Photofinisher's processing peaked at about 1000 films a day and to process these they worked from 7.30am to 4am the following day. Staff enjoyed one week's holiday each year but this could not be taken during the summer months. Bill Holmes found it quite easy to get part-time staff who were prepared to work on a casual basis and he always used student labour during the university vacations. One problem was how to keep things ticking over during the long winter months. He started up as a photographer and took pictures at weddings, christenings, local events and evening dances. He also took photographs of all the local rugby league teams and supplied the pictures in calendars made up in the appropriate team colours. The local National Switch Factory gave them work checking thousands of small switches. This provided them with the means to survive the lean months without losing valuable staff.

Then came flash photography and the 126 Instamatic cameras combined with greater numbers of cheap holiday fights abroad. So things became much easier and the winter months ceased to be a problem.

Bill became a member of WPFA and he found it was a great help to receive their retail price lists and adhere to their recommended terms of business.

In 1962, Bill Holmes started doing colour processing using a Kodak S4 printer and Colortron paper processor. He was joined by his son and was one of the few of the smaller photofinishers who managed to stay independent until he retired in 1996. Despite the intense competition from the late 1970s, they managed to hold their own in an area of the country where a local business giving good service is preferred to the impersonal giants that some of the larger photofinishers had become.

A Scottish Pioneer

Ian Hamilton-Tait, whose parents had bought a retail business selling photographic materials and Meccano in Edinburgh shortly after World War 2, gives another interesting account of how some enterprising finishers built their own equipment when nothing else was available. They soon realised that photo processing was an important part of the business.

In 1947 Ian left school and did his apprenticeship behind the counter and in the small black and white processing department.

The business was successful and in 1949 they moved into much larger premises and started doing black & white D&P for other retailers. This, as with other finishers of that time, was very labour intensive.

In 1954, at the suggestion of Gevaert they started colour processing: first Gevacolor followed by Agfacolor and later Kodacolor C22 negatives. Film and paper processing was done using Fribo hand tanks.

Initially they exposed the colour paper using a borrowed Priox additive single sheet contact printer but soon bought three Leitz Focomat enlargers, which had a drawer for colour filters. With hit and miss grading they were able to expose 40–50 prints per hour including test prints, but the finished output was much less. This was insufficient for their requirements and with no commercial printers on the market, they set out to produce their own equipment.

They adapted a Kodak VPP black and white projection printer for colour work by fitting a rotating filter wheel with blue, green and red printing filters in front of the lamp. Using three variable transformers to switch the lamp to different intensities while projecting through the different colour filters, they were able to control the exposure and colour balance of the prints. Colour grading was largely guesswork and dependent on the experience of the operator. This was made more difficult by the considerable variations between batches of films and papers.

Their first attempt at something better was to use a Pakolor grader, which measured the density of the colour negative films through blue, green and red filters. This improved the pass rate of prints but was still very slow.

To process their rolls of paper they installed a Williamson single-track paper processor specially adapted for Gevacolor paper. Later they added a glazing drum to avoid having to put wet paper on a glazer manually, a common practice at that time.

By 1956 they had the idea of speeding up production by controlling the printers with a five-hole punched tape, similar to those used for telex machines. After processing and grading, a tape was produced for each film. They called this ALEC (Automated Line Equipment Control).

Business was growing, so in 1958 they moved into a purpose-built lab in Penicuik near Edinburgh. They installed Wainco dip and dunk processors for the films and a Kodak three-strand processor for the colour paper. They also took delivery of six English Kodak S1 printers, which was a big step forward as these printers incorporated colour and exposure control.

They gave serious thoughts to adapting their ALEC system to these printers, both to speed up their operation and to integrate them with their invoicing and accounting system. At that time there were many roll films, 120, 126, 127 and 828, so they decided to splice them together and punch a small hole near the edge of each frame to act as a location so that they could transport the films automatically through the S1 printers, correcting the exposures where necessary by means of the punched tape. The idea was also to use the printing information for invoicing using an early computer. The system speeded up the S1 printers from 400 to 600 prints per hour.

They tried to sell the system to other finishers, but it was a system before its time, made obsolete by the much faster colour printers which came on the market a few years later. Interestingly, systems incorporating some of the ideas from ALEC were produced some years later by Gretag and others, for handling re-orders.

Boots

A major influence in UK finishing was a retailer, which was founded in the 19th century. Boots the Chemists eventually had more than 1,600 shops and took D&P very seriously. They accepted D&P from 1920, by which time they had 600 branches. In the first place they established their own Boots brand and they were very demanding, as regards quality and service, of the photofinishers who did their processing. They advertised that their processing was of a superior standard. It was an irony that in many high streets most of the chemists, including Boots, were supplied by the same photofinisher, but the public believed that if you were looking for quality, then you should take your film to Boots. This was very effective and for many years Boots had more than 25% of the total market.

The effect of this was two-fold. Due to the large amount of work, a Boots account was very valuable to photofinishers and this gave them a very strong grip on the market. They used this to control prices as well as a few other things. This must have been one of the earlier examples in the photographic world, of the power of a multiple retailer. At one time Boots used a large number of finishers from all over the country, but in later years they reduced the number to a very few.

Stan Carr, who started in business in 1948, recounts some of what went on. He and his wife set up as wedding photographers in the East End of London. That part of London, badly bombed during the war, was not the easiest place to start a business, so, in addition, they did developing and printing for a few shops. [1] The story he tells would probably mirror how many of the photofinishers were started by hard-working, determined enthusiasts without much capital, or experience of photography. They expanded the numbers of their dealers by offering a 24 hour service at a time when in that part of London, it usually took a week to develop and print black and white films. They built up a nice business, started colour in the early 1960s and eventually acquired a Boots account.

Controlling the Market

In the mid 1950s, Stan joined the WPFA, which he says was a very cosy organisation more or less controlled by the big photofinishers, of which there were several, including the Kodak B companies. In 1972 Stan became President of the WPFA and explains how the system worked. Once a year, shortly before the AGM, the President and the Chairman of the Kodak B companies got together to work out a price list for the following year. They then both went to see the Boots photo buyer and by whatever means possible, got him to agree the new price list. Not surprisingly, in those days, the AGM was attended by all members of the WPFA, all of whom were eager to receive the new industry standard price list, which was always approved and thereby, virtually cast in stone. To complete the process, shortly after the new increased prices had been agreed, the manufacturers Kodak, Agfa and Ilford announced new prices for materials, which took back most of the benefits that the photofinishers had gained. Nevertheless, most members were happy with this, as the business was growing rapidly and price competition had been averted. This situation went on until 1972, when the Heath government outlawed price fixing. It is important to remember that what the leaders of very well respected companies were doing was not only legal, but considered to be the norm. If they had not acted like this, they would have been accused of dereliction of duty.

In the 1960s and 1970s, retailers, and Boots in particular, were very anxious to avoid competition from mail-order photofinishing and would not give work to photofinishers who had a mail-order business. Stan Carr suspected that he lost his Boots account because a mischievous competitor dropped a hint to the Boots buyer that, on a visit to the US in 1971, he had shown an interest in mail-order finishing. While that may or may not have been the case, it was symptomatic of that era of UK photofinishing.

A Remarkable Couple

Until it was declared illegal in the early seventies, one of the WPFA's main aims, in conjunction with the photo dealers, was to control prices and discounts. Any retailer or photofinisher who did not abide by this pricing structure, was immediately boycotted and did not survive for long. There were, however, a few people who defied the rest of the industry and two of these were Geoffrey Stead and his wife Edrei. In 1931, at the height of the depression, they started a photographic studio in Leeds in northern England and, to make ends meet, developed and printed customers' films.

At that time contact prints were standard in the industry, but they decided to offer postcard-sized enlargements, normally three times as expensive, at the same price as contact prints. Naturally they were not very popular with other photo shops and finishers in the area. The PDA (Photographic Dealers Association), in conjunction with the WPFA, ensured that very few shops would give them any work. In 1933 they obtained photographic paper suitable for negatives, which at that time was used by "while you wait" photographers operating at fairgrounds and at the sea side.

These negatives had to be enlarged by reflection printing, but very few people knew how to do it. The Steads cut and spooled this into roll films and started a mail-order service, under the name Gratispool, offering a free 120 sized "paper" film, but charging the standard price for developing and printing. The service was promoted through small adverts in local papers and built up a following among price-conscious consumers. The non-standard negative ensured that all the films came back to them. The PDA and WPFA were powerless to do anything about it, except to ban the Steads from the annual trade shows. They carried on with the paper negatives until the early sixties, by which time they had added colour films from Ferrania, Dynacolor and later Kodak, to become one of the UK's larger photofinishers. They were one of the first mail-order photofinishers, and certainly the first company, to offer a free film.

The Steads had built up their business in very difficult times and in 1935, when they ran out of space in Leeds, they opened a new works in Glasgow, from where much of their mail-order work originated. At that time, economic conditions in Glasgow were terrible, with half the population unemployed. They were mystified why each Thursday several girls fainted, and when they investigated, found that Thursday was the day for collecting unemployment pay, a pitifully small sum in those times. In many families, money ran out several days earlier and the girls had fainted from starvation. A very low-cost canteen, 1 penny for a plate of soup, seemed a likely answer, but for those from the very poorest families, even this was too much, so from then on they provided a free mid-day meal for all their staff. In today's affluent society, looking at 1930s family snap-shots, can leave an uncomfortable feeling, wondering whether they were processed by people with empty stomachs.[2]

Another personality in the Gratispool story was Ron Houslip. In 1935 he acquired his interest in photography when, at the age of 12, he won a camera, complete with a Gratispool paper film. In 1945, after the war, he and a friend started a small lab, but sold it a few years later when his partner decided to join his father's business. Afterwards he worked for various photographic businesses and in 1963, while working for an advertising agency, managed to get the Gratispool account. He came up with the idea of distributing mailing envelopes rather than using press advertising, to expand Gratispool nationwide. In 1967, with some backing from the Steads, he started his own marketing company called the "Free Film Service" which dropped mailing envelopes through people's letter boxes, with the processing done by Gratispool. This turned out to be very successful and Gratispool's market share rose to about 10% by the early 1970s. He also test-marketed a retail format called Supasnaps which offered nothing but processing, films, albums, frames and simple cameras. Ron's activities became part of Gratispool and he joined them, becoming chairman until it was acquired by 3M in 1981. Supasnaps was very successful, growing to 337 branches before being sold to Dixons in 1986 who, in 1993, sold it to Sketchley, the dry cleaners.

Some years later, Ron started Guernsey Colour, which was one of the few remaining mail-order finishers at the beginning of this century. With about 30 employees, processing about a million films per year, it became the third largest mail-order photofinisher in the UK.

3M who had bought Ferrania, the Italian photographic company, saw Gratispool and the Supasnaps shops as a way of establishing themselves in the UK photographic market. Prior to that, Ferrania had only had a relatively small UK presence, mainly in private label film. They purchased several other labs, closing some, but retaining large labs in Glasgow, Northampton and Reading. This did not work out, probably because the Italian-produced film and paper, together with the US Dynachrome film, could not compete against Kodak, Agfa, Fuji and Konica. In 1989 they sold Gratispool to Hedley Taylor, the management team who had bought Dixons Colour Labs.

Kodak

Another similarity of the UK market to that of the US and in this instance also France, was that Kodak was active as a photofinisher. Initially Kodak may have entered the photofinishing business to provide an efficient service, in order to encourage photography, but over the years it became a very profitable business, not to mention the fact that it locked-in the market for paper and chemicals. This was highlighted by the fact that D&P usually costs more than the price of the film. As the independent photofinishing industry grew, Kodak was frequently attacked for competing with their customers and competitors, such as Ilford and Agfa, certainly used this as an argument to sell their materials.

As we saw earlier, In the late 1920s, in order to protect its market for paper, chemicals and machinery and because many photofinishers had fallen onto hard times, Kodak acquired a 51% stake in about 25 photofinishers, who had run into financial difficulties. These companies, the so-called Kodak B companies, continued to trade under their original names and their control by Kodak was kept very quiet, so as not to upset the rest of the industry. In most cases the original owners, or their heirs, continued in the businesses, usually assisted by a Kodak-appointed manager. In addition, Kodak opened four labs, often referred to as the A companies, to provide services such as enlargements, which the B companies were not equipped to provide. In later years, after colour became widespread, the B companies had the additional function of setting high quality standards for the industry.

After World War 2, Kodak opened a laboratory in Hemel Hempstead to process Kodachrome slides and 8mm and 16mm cine film, prints from slides and then later on Kodacolor processing and printing. At its peak the lab employed about 300 people, but by the mid 1980s it had become very uneconomic and was closed and the Kodachrome processing was transferred to France. This caused some ill-feeling among the shrinking band of Kodachrome users and in the mid 1990s Kodak opened a small Kodachrome lab in Wimbledon. This only lasted a few years due to the continual decline of the Kodachrome market, especially after the Millennium.

Mail Order

Strong opposition by retailers probably explains why, for a long time, Gratispool was the only mail-order finisher of any size. Gratispool, quite large by the end of the 1960s, had for a long time promoted itself through small adverts in local papers and thereafter by word of mouth from satisfied customers. At that time it would have been very difficult for any one else to start up by this method. The capital required, and the time needed to generate a sufficient volume, without any retail business, would have made it completely uneconomic. Subsequently, other mail-order finishers have promoted themselves by distributing mailing envelopes.

Sean Hickey, in the late sixties, started one of the few other large mail-order companies in the UK. He had a shop in Torquay and employed six photographers to take pictures in Pontins holiday camps, the equivalent of the modern cruise ship photographer. Processing and printing of the films was done each night in the back of his shop. To augment his work, he started doing mail order under the name Gainafilm, distributing mailing envelopes in South West England. The business quickly outgrew his premises, so he moved to York Road in the nearby town of Paignton and shortly afterwards changed his trading name to York Photo. The move to Paignton turned out to be more difficult than he had anticipated for a number of reasons, including coping with production, which at one stage resulted in six weeks worth of unopened mail-bags. This created problems with the bank which had financed the move and, as a result, the business was bought by the Nashua Corporation of New Hampshire, who had a number of mail-order photofinishing businesses on the eastern side of the US. Nashua subsequently adopted the York Photo brand in the US.

The business continued to grow and in 1985/6 moved to its present premises in Newton Abbot. Soon afterwards, it bought the Truprint mail-order business in Telford. For some years York and Truprint operated from both sites, but when in the late 1990s the mail-order business started to decline, work was concentrated in the Newton Abbot site.

In 2002 Nashua, for whom photofinishing was only a small part of their business, sold both the US and UK York & Truprint businesses to District Photo, of Beltsville, a suburb of Washington D.C. Subsequently District Photo became by far the largest mail-order photofinisher in the world.

An Industrial Fracas

At the beginning of the 21st century the UK had a few other mail-order finishers, the largest being Grunwick, trading under the name of Bonus Print and several other brands. This company has a special place in UK industrial history, as it was a cause célèbre, resulting in legislation to curb excessive union power, which had been building up for several decades, but which reached a pinnacle during the late 1970s.

Grunwick was founded in 1965 in North West London by George Ward and two friends. Having little capital, they had a struggle to get going. Initially they only did black and white processing, subcontracting colour to Cooper and Pearson, a long-established family firm, who had premises nearby. By 1967 they had built up a sufficient number of dealers to go into colour. In 1968, having seen how Gratispool was doing business, giving away free films, they launched their own under the name Bonuspool. After a few false starts, it became successful and the film volume grew rapidly, quickly making their facilities inadequate. They moved and rented additional premises, but the growth in work still left them short of capacity. At the end of 1973 they merged with their neighbours Cooper and Pearson, so that soon the combined company employed about 500 people.[3]

Many of the staff were of Asian descent, having come to the UK from East Africa, where Uganda, under Idi Amin and neighbouring Kenya, had expelled or threatened them. They had travelled from India at the beginning of the 20th century to build the East African railways and had subsequently settled there.

London was not the easiest place for an immigrant and many were pleased to find work with Grunwick. By and large Grunwick was a reasonable place to work, although the pace in the peak summer months was hectic. The pay, at between £25 and £28 for a 40-hour week was not out of line with other places at that time.[4]

The summer of 1976 was particularly hot and work was streaming in, making conditions trying. On August 20th there was an argument with a supervisor and two workers walked out. These were followed by a few others, and this group then approached a trade union asking for assistance. At that stage trade unions had very few members in the photofinishing industry, especially at Grunwick, where in 1973, after a previous dispute, they had been refused recognition. After some deliberation, the union decided this was a good opportunity to get involved and get their own back on George Ward. Some union officials urged caution, as unions had no rights on behalf of employees who had not been members at the time of a dispute. However that part of London was the home of some very belligerent left-wing organisations, who were looking for a scrap with a successful entrepreneur.

George Ward rejected all negotiations with the union and was supported by most of his staff. The trade union movement organised mass picketing and this soon turned to violence outside the gates of the works. The unions tried to organise boycotts of the postal service and suppliers, but with the assistance of friends, most of whom did not share the political views of the union leaders, the company resisted these attacks on the business. The violence got worse, on several occasions many hundreds of police, defending the premises from attack, battled with large numbers of pickets bussed in by several unions from all over the country. This included the miners union, the experts in "flying pickets" who had brought the country to a halt a few years previously. There were many injuries and arrests. The dispute went on for over a year until the unions gradually lost interest, having achieved nothing.

The labour government of the day, dependent on union support, had a problem. Many of its members supported the union action, in fact, several ministers appeared on the picket line. It was, however, also aware that increasing numbers of the public were becoming fed up with the excessive influence of the union movement on the government and no doubt the daily newspaper and TV pictures of fighting between police and violent pickets, were not doing its public image much good. The whole affair contributed to the defeat of the government in the 1979 election, which brought in Margaret Thatcher, who introduced restrictions on unions, in particular, the right to picket in disputes in which they were not directly involved. This completely changed the economic climate in Britain.

This account of the dispute should not be taken as a judgement of the case, no doubt there are always two sides to any argument. Whatever the rights and wrongs, the Grunwick affair had a major effect on industrial relations and the rights of individuals to build successful businesses.

After the affair, Grunwick moved to large modern premises, where it grew to become the largest lab on a single site in the UK, processing more than 10 million films per annum, mainly mail order. It was a well-run company and for many years has had an excellent reputation for quality. Early into this century the company was still private and George Ward has shown himself to be a shrewd operator, remaining one of the few independent photofinishers.[5]

The UK probably has the largest share of mail-order photofinishing of any developed country, reaching about 40% at its peak. This is due to a combination of circumstances. Generally the postal service is fairly good and not too expensive and in contrast to some countries, many people will trust it sufficiently to send their films. For many years retail prices for D&P were fairly high, but due to the fierce competition between finishers, retail margins increased, sometimes to as much as 60%, while finishers costs increased by having to provide an overnight service. This produced a very strong incentive for mail-order finishers, which grew rapidly. Many of them also went in for special promotions with petrol stations and other non-photographic retailers. Eventually retail prices dropped, as did the share of mail order, but it is still higher than in many other countries.

Consolidation

As in other countries, the move into colour triggered consolidation of the several hundred labs that were in business in 1960. One of the first moves was the formation of Northern Associated Photofinishers. Over a period of years, starting in the early 1960s, Charles Plant, a very persuasive individual, got the owners of more than 40 small photofinishers to exchange their businesses for a share of Northern Associated Photofinishers, sometimes called NAP and trading as Napcolour. The bait for this was to become a part owner of a large colour lab in Manchester, with expensive Pako equipment, financed by bank loans supported by Gevaert, in return for Napcolour agreeing to use only their materials. This was probably the first example in the UK of a supplier-financed photofinisher. Nine Pako printers plus the appropriate film and paper processors, together with the WPFA approved price list, was certainly a winning formula, at least for a while.

At one stage NAP had a very large number of shareholder directors and, not surprisingly, some had difficulty in fitting into an organisation, which was much larger than the businesses they had contributed

After some years, the tie with Gevaert became irksome and Charterhouse, a merchant bank, took a 25% stake and provided finance, thereby eliminating the need for the tie to Gevaert. NAP grew to a considerable size, purchasing at least six other labs, four from the Rank Organisation, who at one time had gone into amateur D&P, possibly thinking it was a natural extension of cine film processing. By the end of the 1970s NAP operated from sixteen sites and employed over 1,100 people, probably more in the peak season.

At the same time, Stan Adams who had started his black and white lab in the south, after World War 2, put together a group called United Photographic Laboratories

Limited. The consolidation was financed and the business eventually owned by London International Group, LIG, better known for its Durex contraceptives. The rationale, given at the time, for LIG's expansion into photofinishing, was that both businesses had the same customers in thousands of chemist shops, including Boots. Whether this ever had any practical significance is questionable.

In the early 1980s, Charterhouse saw the opportunity to exit and NAP was sold to LIG and the merged businesses, under the name ColourCare International, became the dominant force in UK photofinishing. This became a very aggressive, expansive group who by the end of the 1980s had 30 % of the UK market, processing some 28 million films a year. For the next decade ColourCare took over most of the remaining independent photofinishers and also a number of processors working for estate agents and school photographers. They also opened a lab in the north of Norway and tried, unsuccessfully, to take over France's largest group of photofinishers.

Boots, who at one time sent its work to about 60 photofinishers, consolidated to two suppliers, 60% to ColourCare and 40% to Kodak and this triggered further growth for these two groups. ColourCare, who had acquired a mail-order company on the south coast, were forced to restrict their mail-order business to outside the UK in order to keep their Boots contract. For several years their lab in Deal, Kent did mail-order finishing for French and Scandinavian customers, countries where photofinishing was much more expensive than in the UK.

Dixons, which was the UK's largest photo retailer, went into photofinishing in 1967, purchasing a lab in Stevenage. Some time later, they took over Agfa's reversal film lab in Wimbledon and two other labs, in Rugely and in Telford, the latter specialising in 35 mm mail-order processing. In 1986, Dixons bought the 337 Supasnaps shops and Gratispool's labs in Glasgow, Reading and Northampton from 3M, the remaining Gratispool labs having meanwhile been closed. At its peak in the late 1980s, Dixons Colour Labs were processing 26 million rolls of film per annum out of a UK total of about 102 million rolls.

In 1989, Dixons decided to concentrate on retail and sold its photofinishing labs to its management, who closed the Stevenage lab and moved all its mail-order finishing, operating under the Truprint brand, to the Telford lab. A few months later, in 1990, the wholesale labs in Glasgow, Northampton, Rugely, Reading and Wimbledon, were bought by Kodak and the Telford mail-order lab was sold to Nashua (York Photo).

Up to the end of the 1980s the Kodak B companies, operating under their original names, were a fairly low-key operation. It appeared to an outside observer, that some of the Kodak management were afraid to admit to the industry that Kodak was seriously involved in the photofinishing business.

In 1990, this changed after Kodak had bought the five large labs that had previously belonged to Dixons and merged these with their B companies, which had become 100% owned subsidiaries, to form KPC, Kodak Processing Companies. Competing with their customers was no longer an issue, Kodak were now quite openly in the photofinishing business, aggressively competing for a large market share.

Boots had become ever more demanding and from the early 1980s had forced both Kodak and ColourCare to install and operate minilabs in their larger branches. At the end of each day, any work not completed in the shops was collected for overnight processing by the nearest Kodak or ColourCare lab.

An interesting point was that Boots, to maintain their brand, forced both ColourCare and Kodak to collect and deliver to the shops in plain white vans. It must have been a blow to ColourCare who had spent years building up their brand.

By the late 1990s things started going wrong at ColourCare. Intense competition from mail order, pressure from Boots, problems in Norway, plus a change in the estate agents market, put them into a loss situation. Nobody had any idea of how to solve the problem and LIG, who also had problems in other parts of its business, sold ColourCare to its management for a nominal sum, giving them a loan as working capital. The new owners quickly cut costs, sold off the overseas mail-order business and then sold the business to other members of the management. In 2002, the remnants of ColorCare, but now without a Boots contract, were bought by Kodak.

An interesting point was the reaction of the UK competition authorities who have to approve every merger in which any one party acquires a predominant market share. By this time there were not too many wholesale photofinishers left who could operate on a national scale and those who remained were not interested in the Boots business. This had become very difficult, and Kodak was left with a tricky task to keep it profitable, but more of that later. The condition for the merger to be approved, was to spin-off the ColourCare and Kodak delivery organisations into a separate independent business, which would accept work from any finisher on similar terms. The result of this was that some small finishers were able to accept work from anywhere, as long as it was in the delivery area of the national distribution company. This has allowed a number of specialist finishers doing, for example, black and white or transparency processing, to solicit work from all over the country.

Other Interesting Facts

There have been a few other interesting developments. There were several finishers with their own retail outlets. Foto Processing had been a very small wholesale photofinisher in Bradford, but when Martin Hemsworth, the son of the founder, took over in the early 1980s, he terminated the contracts of all of his dealers and started opening his own shops. Within quite a short time he had about 90 outlets and was processing over three million films per annum from a modern works in Leeds. The business was based on good retail locations, low prices, and efficient working. Foto Processing was a very economical operation, working round the clock, having avoided getting into the rat race which had been created by the overnight service operated by both Kodak and ColourCare. As a comparison, one of ColourCare's larger works, also processing three million films per annum, had to collect from over 1200 shops each day and work at night, with the lab standing idle during the day. Unfortunately, after Martin withdrew from the business, it ceased to be so successful.

A similar type of business was Klick Photopoint in Wishaw, Scotland, which combined its photofinishing with dry cleaning and that, no doubt, reduced the costs of its shops and transport. By the Millennium they had become very large, having taken over Foto Processing and two other finishers with their own shops, Max Spielman and Orbit, who had both been successful in their time.

That left only one other large player in the UK in 2003. Naresh Patel had a successful photo business in Nairobi, Kenya, which he equipped with UK manufactured Colortron colour printing and processing equipment, in the mid 1960s. He tells an interesting story of how he coped with the shortage of skilled people. The Asians, of whom there were not too many, did all the critical jobs, while the carrying and fetching was left to the Africans. Film processing was done in a hand line, the critical part, which consisted of handling the films in the developer tank, being an Asian task with a number of Africans doing the rest. It is no surprise that much of Africa has problems, now that many Asians and Europeans have left.

Naresh Patel came to London in the 1970s and, after opening a shop in Greenwich, founded the Colorama processing lab in central London. It prospered very quickly, possibly helped by the fact that many film drop-off points, such as chemists and newsagents, were run by Asian immigrants, who could relate better to a fellow immigrant than the "slightly superior" and impersonal Kodak or ColourCare. To add to its clout of very competitive prices, Colorama offered a same-day service, "in by 10, out by 4", in central London. Within a few years it was processing six million films a year, making it one of the largest labs in the UK. Colorama has become part of a much larger group, including a pharmaceutical wholesaler, with whom it shares some of the distribution and this, no doubt, cuts costs. At a later stage, they also opened a second lab in Manchester, but this has never been as successful as the London lab.

Other Well-known Names

In this account of photofinishing in the UK, there has been very little mention of some other well-known names in photography.

In the 1930s and the immediate post war years, Ilford were very strong in B&W films and Kennington and Bourlet, a subsidiary, produced photofinishing equipment. In addition they were involved in several colour processes for which they set up their own lab. Dufaycolor was one of the first colour processes available to amateurs and in the 1950s and early 1960s, they followed this with Ilfachrome transparencies and the Ilfacolor print process. None of these were released to independent photofinishers because Ilford had found it difficult enough to produce consistent results in their own extensive lab. There were, no doubt, considerable batch variations in the films, which made life difficult.

Ilfacolor 35mm negative film was interesting as it was sold process-paid including a strip of contact prints. The processed negatives in cardboard mounts, similar to those used for transparencies, together with the contact strip, were returned to the customer, who then sent those he wanted printed, to Ilford. Not so different perhaps to what happens with digital images?

Ilford's colour films came to an end as a result of a rather perverse ruling of the Monopolies Commission in 1965. David Willey, the owner of Munns Brothers lab in Birmingham together with some other stalwarts of the WPFA, had complained to the government that Kodachrome was sold process-paid and therefore excluded independent photofinishers, a re-run of what had led to the consent decree in the US a decade earlier. The Monopolies Commission not only made this illegal, but also ruled that Kodak had established a monopoly in colour photography that was making excessive profits, which was against the public interest. They then made Kodak reduce their prices, with the result that both Ilford and Agfa found it uneconomic to compete and so they withdrew many of their films and services so that Kodak's market share increased even more.

After the Monopolies Commission ruling, Ilford continued to supply their colour negative films to FCA, the Film Corporation of America, which was a large mail-order finisher operating both in the US and several European countries. FCA went out of business a few years later with Ilford being a substantial creditor.

David Willey was one of the very few to start processing Kodachrome, but soon gave up after making large losses.

Agfa colour films were introduced in the UK in the early 1950s. For the process-paid transparency films, Agfa established their own laboratory in Wimbledon, while the negative print films were handled by five designated independent finishers. After the 1965 Monopolies Commission ruling, their films went very much in decline until, some years later, they released films compatible with Kodak's processes.

Agfa have always produced excellent photofinishing equipment and they actively marketed that in the UK, particularly after their merger with Gevaert, when the sale of Pako equipment declined. They used every possible marketing ploy and it is probably no coincidence that two of the largest labs at the Millennium, equipped with some of the most modern Agfa equipment, used Agfa paper and chemicals.

Fuji did not enter the UK photofinishing market, other than appointing a designated lab for their transparency films. Since the early 1980s they had been very active in selling colour paper both on the strength of its quality and price. From the mid 1990s to the early part of this century Kodak has extended its grip on the wholesale photofinishers market, but Fuji have surged ahead in the minilab market. This is highlighted by two events.

In the mid 1990s, Boots changed their policy as regards minilabs. Instead of having Kodak install and operate minilabs in their larger shops, they decided to operate their own. Over a period of about a year, they bought over 500 Fuji minilabs running on Fuji paper and chemicals. This must have been a double blow to Kodak as it deprived them of both finishing volume and paper and chemical sales. The matter will have been made worse since just before the Millennium, when film sales had started declining. This has meant that an ever-increasing proportion of films are being processed in the shops, further reducing the number of films collected by the Kodak wholesale labs.

Cameras, especially of the digital kind, are now sold by a very large variety of outlets. However, Jessops, with over 240 branches in 2003 and likely to grow to many more, has become a major supplier for serious photographers. They operate their own central lab, plus Fuji digital minilabs, in many of their shops.

The number of minilabs, especially of the digital type, continues to grow. Many minilabs are located in supermarkets and chain stores such as Tesco, Sainsbury, Asda, Boots and Jessops and in addition there are several franchise chains.

Many of the free-standing minilabs now carry out a certain amount of professional work and, conversely, most professional labs have a digital minilab and some use these to offer an amateur printing service.

By the end of 2004 the move to digital photography had progressed considerably. Sales of films had dropped quite dramatically and, combined with the increase in the number of minilabs, this meant that a very much higher proportion of the films were processed by retailers. This has made life for the wholesale labs very difficult, particularly for Kodak who claimed that their film-processing volumes had dropped to 30% compared with 2001, making the labs uneconomic. They announced that they would close their remaining six labs by the end of 2005 and had arranged for Bonus Print whose business had been mainly mail order, to provide a service to their retail outlets.

In late 2005 CeWe, the large German photofinishing group, acquired Standard Photographic, who had previously provided UK processing for Fuji transparency films. It was assumed that they would offer similar services to those which they provide in Germany, France and many other European countries.

By mid 2005 there had been a dramatic increase in online photofinishing, no doubt encouraged by the rapid growth in the number of broadband Internet connections.

As in other countries, there is intense competition for printing images from digital cameras. The suppliers of home computer printers, paper and ink cartridges are fighting for market share, with minilabs and online labs suggesting that wholesale labs supplying retailers will disappear before too long. One exception to this might be specialist labs processing black and white and transparency films and other niche work.

1 Stan Carr "From Start to Phinish" Memoirs, August 2002
2 Geoffrey Stead Diary 1932–1964
3 Fort Grunwick by George Ward Temple Smith, Chapter 3
4 Grunwick by Joe Rogaly Penguin, various chapters
5 Fort Grunwick by George Ward Temple Smith Chapter 3, page 20

CHAPTER 8

France

France was one of the birthplaces of photography and photofinishing, as we know it today, started there early in the last century. As everywhere, professional photographers and photo shops did most of the developing and printing for amateurs. This was the pattern for many years and there were very few dedicated photofinishers in the first half of the 20th century.

One of the exceptions was George Eastman who, anxious to spread his activities worldwide, started his French sales company in 1897. In 1901 he visited Paris with a view to building a factory to produce films and papers, but this did not happen for some years. In 1904 he opened two shops and processing laboratories in Paris and soon after that, other labs in Nice and Lyons. In 1913 he built a larger laboratory in Paris to replace one of the earlier labs. The French business had grown and with 100 employees, processed several thousand films per day. By the mid-twenties a new lab in Sevran, near Paris, which had replaced the earlier labs, was processing 30,000 prints per day. In 1921 and 1922 Kodak opened new labs in Nice and Marseilles.

In 1927, the Sevran lab started processing 16mm reversal cine film and was later expanded to process several million rolls of amateur film per annum, but more of that later.

A major player in photography in the earlier part of the century was Charles Pathé whose main interests were cine film and making movies. His company manufactured film and also the necessary equipment, some of which was copied from the Lumiere brothers. By 1908 the Pathé Cinema Company had become the largest photographic company in France employing about 4,500 people.[1] In addition to the film, which they manufactured themselves, they also purchased film from several sources, including Lumiere and Kodak.

For many years the biggest problem was the flammability of the film base and, in common with others, Pathé started research into a non-flammable film base. On the east side of Paris, in the suburb of Vincennes, he built studios and a large factory to manufacture, coat and process non-flammable films. George Eastman, unhappy with large-scale competitors for his films, merged his French business with that of Charles Pathé. Kodak took on the manufacture of films and provided processing, while Pathé concentrated on producing and showing movies. Consequently, the Kodak Pathé Company was formed in 1927 and its Vincennes factory became a major source of photographic material.

Early Pioneers

Prior to World War 2, in addition to Kodak, there were a few other photofinishers, principally those owned by Marcel Hamelle, Marc Contet and Lucien Racine. Marc Contet started as a photographer in 1918 and in 1930 was doing processing for other photographers. In 1931 he joined up with Henri Rozand calling their business Romaphot. His main competitor was Marcel Hamelle.

Marcel Hamelle and his wife started their business in 1926. They worked from the basement of their house in Montrouge, a suburb on the south side of Paris, collecting and delivering to chemists by bicycle. Apparently most of the professional photographers in the area were not interested in D&P because they thought it might compete with their other business. The Hamelles prospered and by the time Marc Contet started processing a few years later, they were employing 10 people. They competed fiercely but later became close friends. In 1934 Marcel Hamelle, who must have been very enterprising, bought 1000 Brownie box cameras from Kodak in London and gave them to opticians to loan to customers who wanted to experience photography. This was a very successful promotion and probably explains why in France opticians became much more important than pharmacies for film sales and developing and printing.

Marcel's son Roger joined his father in 1952 and three years later they started processing Gevacolor colour transparency films. The business grew rapidly and in 1955 they built a 6,000 square metre lab housed in a six-story building in Montrouge. It became the largest lab in France, possibly even in Europe. It was very impressive to see its 80 colour printers laid out in eight rows of ten, when many other labs were proud to have 10 or less printers. The lab was large, not only because of the amount of work, but also due to the fact that, for a number of years from the late 1950s, there were so many different colour processes which each required to be handled separately. At one time they had set up for three transparency and several negative processes in addition to black and white. This was in contrast to the United States, where because of its strong market position, most finishers only handled Kodak processes.[2]

Roger Hamelle remembers that, in the early days of colour, they were lucky if an operator could expose 1000 prints per day compared to the 20,000 prints per hour of a colour printer in the 1990s. At the beginning of colour, they, like many of the other pioneers, built some of their own equipment. Most of the business was in the Paris region, but they also served retailers in other parts of France by mail. During the early 1980s they tested a Gretag minilab at Carrefour. He described it as their "Concorde" service, very fast and very expensive". It did not catch on, the equipment was too complicated for retail use. It was, in fact, some years ahead of its time.[3]

During the 1970s and 1980s, sales of colour films grew rapidly and this, together with developments in processing and printing technology, meant that labs had to make considerable investments to stay competitive. Productivity, for the best equipped and organised labs, rose rapidly and this presented problems for some, in particular for those with too many staff. Hamelle had over expanded and for a number of reasons got into financial trouble, failing in the mid 1980s. At its peak of operation he employed about 550 people, probably 200 more than he needed. French laws and the unions made it very difficult to dismiss surplus staff except by closing a business. Hamelle was unable or unwilling to act like some of his competitors, who solved the problem by purchasing or starting a new lab some distance away, closing the existing one and offering the staff a job at the new business. Most would not accept such a move and thereby lost their job with only a moderate payoff.

As we have seen, colour labs started in the early 1950s. Atlanticolor was believed to be the first in 1951 and others followed soon after. There was a rapid expansion and by the beginning of the 1970s there were about 300 labs, some of which were quite sizeable, the largest being the Paris lab of Marcelle Hamelle. After that there were many amalgamations, so that by the 1980s the number had halved and by the end of the century there were less than 70 labs, most owned by five groups, Kodak, Fuji, Spector, CEWE and Konica, with a few smaller independents.

The French market differed from that of some other countries, in that the retail end was largely based on professional photographers. The amateurs were in the main enthusiasts, rather than snap-shooters and this encouraged high-quality work at high prices. One of the results of this was that French finishers used very nice but expensive packaging for their work. In the 1960s and 1970s there were hardly any pharmacy or drugstore outlets, in particular no chains, such as in the UK and the US. There was relatively little price competition among the labs and this encouraged many start-ups.

LLA and Racine

Despite the fact that France has a big concentration of its population in the vicinity of Paris, many of the larger labs were based outside the city where costs were considerably lower. In 1961, after a visit to the US several of the larger labs in the four opposite corners of France formed LLA (Les Laboratoires Associés). Initially it was a friendly club which shared information on prices, suppliers' discounts and technology. It soon developed into an organisation which divided up the French market between the four groups, each consisting of several labs. Nominally the groups each traded in a separate segment of the country centred on Paris. However, there was a certain amount of distrust, caused among other things, by poaching each other's territories. Over the years, as the competition from other groups built up, it became a financially connected group owned by a few flamboyant families. At its peak it consisted of 22 labs and controlled about 35% of the French market.

One of the driving forces of LLA, Guy Strittmatter, whose business, Labo Service Normandie, was based in Caen, tragically died in 1982 following a car crash. The best years were past and in 1988 the main shareholders decided they did not want to carry on and so put the business up for sale. There was bidding from several companies, including Fuji and ColourCare of the UK, but eventually Kodak bought the business for more than FFr 450 million ($m75). This raised Kodak's market share to above 50%, a situation which would not have been tolerated in many other countries.

The Racine group consisted of a number of labs all over France linked by some rather convoluted financial arrangements. It was put together by Serge Buga who had learned his photofinishing from Claude Bloch, with his Opéco lab. In 1973 he bought the Racine lab in Paris from the elderly sons of the founder. It had been in business since 1930, but was no longer doing very well. An amusing story is told that the 75 year old sons could not face up to telling Mme Racine, their 95 year old mother, that they had sold the business. She still lived in the apartment above the lab and every evening the day's receipts, since all business was for cash, were taken up to her before being passed to Serge. [4] Serge Buga very quickly revived the business and acquired several more struggling labs in the Paris region, having been helped by his friends at Agfa with market information to assist him in purchasing them on advantageous terms.

By that time, as a result of the move to colour and increasing price competition, there were a number of mergers and takeovers, in many cases involving the LLA group. Buga persuaded several owners of regional labs of the desirability of consolidation and formed a loose alliance with them to create the Racine Group which eventually served most of France.

Serge Buga did business with trade unions, who had several hundred thousand members, plus families, at Renault and other factories. The unions, who had tax-free status, were allowed to trade and use the proceeds to finance themselves. He set up union shops inside the factories offering them low retail prices, but also low discounts, so that Racine's net prices were very good. This put pressure on more traditional retail outlets, which in turn created problems for other labs, particularly Hamelle.

When the Hamelle lab went out of business, Serge Buga acquired the six-story building in Montrouge and shortly afterwards got together with Marc Contet of Romaphot, who had taken over from his father in 1973 and also with Claude Bloch and his Opéco lab. Between them they now owned a number of labs in the Paris region, some of which they closed, thereby getting rid of surplus staff while retaining the customers.

They were very creative in their marketing. After the 126 Instamatic films were launched in 1963, Claude Bloch went to Carrefour, the chain of hypermarkets who had not been an outlet for processing, and introduced the bonus print. This consisted of a small print in addition to the normal print plus a Carrefour logo. Carrefour used these for promotions, which were based on the collection of these logos.

Jean-Claude and Pierre Rosenblum, who had had a variety of photographic businesses, brought them an interesting source of processing in exchange for a small share in Racine. The distribution of newspapers and magazines to more than 16,000 shops and kiosks throughout France was in the hands of one company. The brothers organised the sale of films and the collection of processing through the distribution network of this company. Although the number of processing orders collected per outlet was small, the total was considerable and using the newspaper delivery system was very cost-effective. The news stands, which sold newspapers with an 8% margin were happy to receive 15% per order, which was considerably less than the 50% or more which the labs normally gave to shops.

Racine, like many of the other labs during the early 1980s, had experimented with minilabs but this had not been very successful. The idea was to supply these to their larger retailers so that they could provide a one-hour service and thereby increase their business. There were considerable difficulties, a combination of high costs, and probably more importantly, the early minilabs required a higher degree of skill than most retailers could, or were willing to, provide. In the late 1980s a Californian company, Photogo with their "Imager", seemed to provide a way round this. The Photogo microlab was in fact a second attempt to introduce a Kis designed product. Although a great improvement on the earlier Kis machines, it was considerably less expensive than those provided by Japanese manufacturers, such as Noritsu, but apparently capable of producing good-quality results. With its terrible reputation from a few years earlier, the Kis connection was carefully disguised.

Being aware of the disastrous results of earlier days, Racine did extensive tests, which convinced them that the Photogo Imager was a viable proposition for one-hour retail photo processing. They purchased 250 Photogo Imagers for their more remote retailers to allow them to compete with the minilabs, which were beginning to spring up. It quickly became apparent that the Imager was quite unsuitable for this purpose. It had worked well when operated by Racine's own well-trained staff, but when put in the hands of retailers, for whom it was a marginal activity, it was not very good.

To make matters worse, Kodak Fuji and Agfa had been busy introducing new films so there were now a considerable variety of colour negative films on the market. They were all supposed to use the Kodak process, but their printing characteristics were very different. Large photofinishers, using expensive colour printers and with highly trained QC staff, could cope with this, but not the shops to which Racine had supplied the Photogo Imagers. Racine had to take back the machines, Photogo washed their hands of the affair and Racine suffered a substantial loss.

Spector

The Racine group had a considerable share of the French market, since by the early 1990s, the Paris lab was processing in excess of five million films per annum, far more than any other lab in France. The provincial Racine labs, although much smaller, were processing a further nine – ten million films. During the early 1990s the price of colour prints dropped considerably and this made it difficult for the Racine group to keep their labs updated and stay competitive. The Racine Group was very important to Agfa, who supplied their materials and equipment and when things became difficult, supported them with generous credit. Eventually in 1994 the business was sold to Spector, a very go-ahead Belgium group, who had been doing mail-order finishing in France from their Belgium lab. Spector who had been very successful and, having raised considerable sums on the Brussels stock exchange, decided to modernise the Racine facilities. In a very short time they built an ultramodern lab to replace the very old Paris facility. When it opened in 1995, it was equipped with the most advanced machinery and systems available. It was a showplace, probably unique in the world at the time. Spector also modernised the remaining Racine labs in the rest of France. They dramatically reduced the costs, drove hard bargains, switched suppliers and thereby almost halved the cost of their paper and chemicals. Agfa lost a large part of their French market.

For a few years Spector was very successful in France. However, they also moved into Germany where they ran into serious problems which threatened to bring down the whole group and, as a result, they sold the French labs to Kodak in 2001. This was the second time in a decade and a half that Kodak had obtained an enormous market share in France. The sale created turmoil in the market and some of the customers, such as the newspaper stands brought to Racine and then Spector by the Rosenblum brothers, switched to one of the other groups. It did not take very long for Kodak to lose a sizeable proportion of the customers it had gained.

For a short period 3M, who had bought Ferrania, the Italian photographic manufacturer, operated a number of labs in France in the hope of creating a market for its films and colour paper, but this did not work and the labs were then sold.

With so many mergers taking place, another smaller informal group was formed in 1972. Called LPFR, Laboratoires Photographiques France Region, it originally consisted of seven labs but was later joined by others. LPFR lasted until the mid 1990s, but over the years most were acquired by one of the larger groups or went out of business.

Fuji

The story of Fuji in France, which by the end of 2003, was considered by many to be the market leader, is closely connected with the Develay family. When Fuji first came to Europe in the early 1960s, it did not set up its own subsidiaries in France and the sale of Fuji products was instead undertaken by Mr René Develay and his wife Jaqueline. In 1975 they and Fuji decided that they should open their first lab near Paris. Its main purpose was to process the process-paid reversal films, in particular the Single 8 cine film, which had become very successful. Six years later they opened a second lab in the south near Marseilles. The labs were run by their son Claude, together with his wife Catherine, who have continued to manage the business into the 21st century. The French agency, together with the labs, became part of Fuji Photo Film in 1996.

Fuji had been one of the bidders for LLA and when this failed, they opened or purchased five more labs in Lille, Toulouse, Lyon, Sarguemines and Rennes within a period of one year, giving them a major share of the French market. They continued to expand, buying five more labs and building one more in Caen in the period up to 1995. The build-up has been impressive. By the end of 2000 the 13 labs were processing some 25 million rolls of colour negative film and by August 2003, when there were only three groups of wholesale labs in France, their share of the market, excluding minilabs was about 38%. Their steady growth was in marked contrast to LSK, Labo Service Kodak, where there has been continuous turmoil and reorganisation ever since the purchase of LLA in 1988.

CeWe

This leaves only one other major among the wholesale labs. In the mid 1970s, CeWe, the German lab group, opened an office in Lille, Northern France and started delivering to non-traditional outlets such as hypermarkets. CeWe's costs were very much lower than French labs, but due to the distances over which they had to collect and deliver, business was on a relatively small scale and did not create much of a threat to the French industry. In 1986, CeWe decided to make a serious move into the French market and bought a Paris lab, which they set about modernising and bringing up to the standards of their German labs. Their main thrust was into the low-cost market, in particular Photo Station, a chain of shops, which sell only films and processing at prices low by French standards. As Photo Station grew to 300 shops, CeWe acquired a further seven labs culminating with the Konica lab in Paris in 2001.[5]

CeWe Color has moved very seriously into the digital image market and, by the end of 2003, this was expected to account for 20% of the total work and was still growing rapidly. Much of this work came from kiosks installed in Photo Station or similar outlets or from orders placed via the Internet from the sites of their retail customers.

By early this century the French market had become very competitive, with the three groups, Fuji, CeWe and Kodak competing fiercely. Kodak, with its purchase of the very modern Spector labs, should have had a commanding position but, as film sales began to decrease, its market share began to drop much faster than that of the other two groups. By the end of 2003 Kodak had announced several lab closures and two years later was down to two labs, with a further lab expected to close before the end of 2006. Fuji and CeWe appeared to be doing much better, although they have also reduced the number of labs, but nobody can predict how the large wholesale labs will evolve in later years as printing from digital cameras becomes ever more important.

Mail-order photofinishing has never caught on in France probably because many people distrust the post and it's high cost. At one time there were principally three companies; Maxicolor, Spector and Photo Labo Club. At various times these companies did the actual processing outside France where they were able to operate at lower costs. Their market share fluctuated between 2% and 3%, which is very much less than in the UK and Scandinavia.

Minilabs

Minilabs initially had a difficult time. Some labs like Hamelle and others tried, without much success, to install retail minilabs in the early 1980s. Then, in the mid 1980s came the episode of the first generation Kis minilabs, sold very aggressively to shopkeepers with no experience of processing. Anybody with the slightest experience of colour printing knew that they did not work, but that did not stop several hundred people from parting with their money, never to see a return. Just to rub it in, the experienced Racine group did not fare any better with the Photogo Imagers. It is not surprising that many labs and others from the French photographic establishment decreed that retail minilabs were not a good idea. For a long time Kodak said that minilabs would not work in France, but even they could not stop them for ever.

Technology moved on and so eventually the case for minilabs was made. By the end of 2003 there were 3000–4000 minilabs in France, half in hypermarkets or similar outlets. They account for 30%, possibly more, of the total market and this is almost certainly growing. The biggest and most successful group of free-standing minilabs, with over 200 outlets in France is Photo Service. They produce high quality at top prices and often include a small studio. There are a few other chains each with 30–50 outlets. In addition, the film manufacturers each have branded chains, but the outlets are individually owned. Estimates suggest that there are about 150 Kodak Express labs and about 300 each of Agfa and Fuji branded labs.

Many of the free-standing labs are equipped with digital minilabs, which are capable of the highest quality results. A good number of these are operated by professional photographers who often combine amateur processing with a portrait studio and some wedding photography.

The rapid increase in digital cameras and the reduction in films have created severe problems for the French industry in persuading the snap-shooter to bring his images for printing. Considerable effort is going into reducing costs and making enticing offers. For example, the Fuji labs have introduced the very attractive-looking 6 x 8 cm "Pocket Photo" packed in 25s, 50s, 100s and eventually in 1,000s.

The widespread use of the Internet, especially broadband, has brought on-line photofinishing, the modern version of mail order, to France. By 2006 there were two fairly large on-line finishers, Photoways and myPIXmania, plus a number smaller labs. In addition, both Fuji and CeWe were accepting on-line work, but delivering via their retail outlets.

We have seen earlier how the Rosenblum brothers, Pierre and Jean-Claude, were active in selling photofinishing, in addition to numerous other photo businesses. By early this century, Jean-Claude's sons Steve and Jean-Emile had taken over and were busy expanding a web-based photographic business which included myPIXmania, the on-line finisher, a chain of 250 retail outlets, many with minilabs and school and baby photographers.[6] In 2006, DSG the parent company of the UK group of Dixons, bought a majority share in the business.

1 Pierre Clement Pioneers of the French Photographic Industry, IS&T 1985
2 Meeting and telphone discussion with Roger Hamelle, July and October 2003
3 Meeting and telephone discussion with Roger Hamelle, July and October 2003
4 Star Press Group, European Professional Imaging Millennium Edition, page 85
5 CEWE Historical notes and 2001 accounts
6 See http://www.fotovista.com

CHAPTER 9

Italy

Italy has a long tradition of photography and for many years Ferrania, named after the small town in northern Italy where it is based, has manufactured cine and still films as well as photographic papers. Up to the 1950s, most photography was in black and white and developing and printing was carried out by photo shops and professional photographers.

Ferrania was the market leader and in the 1950s introduced colour transparencies, followed by colour negatives and prints. However, there were few labs available to process and print them. In the 1960s Kodak introduced its colour films to the Italian market and shortly afterwards was followed by Agfa. Soon Kodak became the market leader and opened a large lab in Milan plus 10–12 independent affiliated labs which were tightly controlled through the restricted supply of 3½” (89 mm) wide rolls of colour paper. Similar tactics have been employed in other countries. In reply, Agfa launched 25 franchised Agfacolor Service Labs.

Colour slides and 8mm cine in both black and white and colour were very popular and were sold process-paid. Ferrania, Agfa and Kodak had captive labs to process these in Milan, Rome and Palermo.

Photography, and thus photofinishing, were helped by the availability of stylish cameras which were produced by both Ferrania and Bencini.

The film manufacturers controlled the photographic market including processing. Kodak and Agfa achieved this by offering their labs very long payment terms for equipment in return for exclusive paper and chemical contracts and this restricted the labs’ pricing and choice of retail outlets. Prices for processing were at that time very high. The improved colour films, and in particular the 126 Instamatic films, gave the industry and especially Kodak a boost.

During the 1960s Ferrania was bought by 3M and, as far as amateur products are concerned, became almost exclusively a private label producer of films for sale by chains such as Boots and Supasnap in the UK and others in France, Germany and the US. Ferrania did make an attempt to enter the photofinishing business in the UK and France, but abandoned this after a few years.

The Equipment Industry

The 1970s were a time of rapid expansion for a number of Italian manufacturers of photofinishing equipment. By the end of the decade, names such as San Marco, Safai, Afi, Polielettronica, Technolab, Systel, GPE, Fotoba, Rollma LED, Barbieri and Filmeccanica became well known for a wide range of small-scale photofinishing equipment.

Small labs with four or five employees opened all over the country, especially in the tourist areas. These small labs were quite important, as Italian unions were very restrictive for businesses employing more than 15 people. By the end of the decade some had grown to 40–50 staff and were processing 100,000–200,000 films per annum. A few labs were considerably larger, although compared to other European countries, Italian labs tended to be smaller.

The better known names among the labs included Ramero, Garetto, FLT, Color Record, Color Service, Giuman, Color Color, Gregoris, Galotti, Villani, Art Color, Super Color, MC Film, Civiletti, Fiorito and Arpa.

Photography was growing rapidly and by 1980 had reached 40 million rolls per annum, of which about 30 million were colour negative, the rest equally spread between colour transparencies and black and white. The increase in silver prices may have helped the growth of colour photography as it is less affected by the cost of silver compared to black and white films. Kodak's share of the market was about 60%.

Surprisingly, Italy adopted strict environmental laws much earlier than some other countries and the recycling of photographic chemicals became quite common. One reason for this may have been that in many areas the sewage systems were not equipped to handle photographic waste, particularly silver, and hence labs had to install recycling systems in order to avoid dumping it into the sewers. The capital expenditure to do this forced some labs out of business.

The union situation became more difficult in the 1980s and as a result Kodak closed its large lab in Milan. Some independent labs processed one million films per annum, but due to high distribution costs, no national chains of labs came into being. By the end of the 1980s there were 90–100 medium sized labs and some 1200 minilabs processing about 64 million rolls of film.

The growth of colour photography continued during the 1990s, reaching about 90 million rolls by the Millennium, of which only 5% were transparencies. During the mid 1990s there were over 100 photofinishers, many processing 300,000–400,000 rolls per annum. In addition, there were some 3,500 minilabs.

There was further concentration among the photofinishers towards the end of the decade so that numbers were down to 94 in 1999, 60 in 2001 and 45 in 2002. There have been many mergers and by 2002 there were three big groups.

In northern Italy a group of five labs processed about eight million rolls; in the centre nine labs processed seven million rolls; and in the south six labs processed six million rolls. These three groups controlled about 30% of the 80 million rolls market. The balance of some 48 million rolls was processed by 4,200 minilabs and 25 smaller labs, of which only two have a capacity of 200,000–300,000 rolls per annum. The reason for quoting these figures is to illustrate how the Italian market differs from most other European countries where the small labs have disappeared and most of the remaining labs now process several million rolls per annum.

Subsequently, as in other countries, there has been a sharp decline in the number of films sold. By 2005 they had dropped to less than 35 million, well under half the number before digital cameras became popular. This has had a corresponding effect on the remaining labs, where the printing of digital images has not compensated for the reduction in the number of films. The main groups such as Rikorda, Vitros and Fincolor have absorbed other labs and, together with Art Color, Fotocine Meridionale and Print Center, form the remaining wholesale photofinishers.

In recent years there has been a change in the distribution methods. By 2005 some 30% of processing was through mass merchandisers while minilabs accounted for about 60%. The Italian market is far more fragmented than in other European countries, 90% of the minilabs are run by independent operators, with only a few small chains run by Foto Color House, Foto Magiche and Foto Fly. The hypermarkets do not seem to have purchased minilabs although a few may have made their big lab suppliers install them.

By 2006 there were a few on-line labs, such as Photo City, taking business via the Internet, but it does not yet seem to be on a very large scale.

Another characteristic of the Italian photofinisher market is the regional variation in price and quality. Prices in the poorer areas of the south have sometimes been half that of the prosperous north.

As always, the operations of the processing labs are related to the sale of films or digital cameras. The latter have increased from about 100,000 in 2000 to over 2,500,000 in 2005. This included 75,000 single lens digital reflex cameras.

Much of this information was provided by Giulio Forte, Editor of Reflex Magazine. g.forti@reflex.it
Some of the data is from A.I.F., Associazione Italiana Fotocine.

CHAPTER 10

Germany

The overriding characteristic of the German photofinishing industry has been QUALITY. Germany has had a tradition of the "Meister", the master craftsmen, apprentice-trained and proud of the fact that whatever they do, is to the highest possible standard. This is in contrast to the English, who for many years lauded the gifted amateur, by definition a self taught person, who is often at the top of his chosen craft but where there were always others, whose standards were rather lower.

This soon showed up in photography where, for the first 60 years from 1841, there was no developing and printing service as such and where amateurs, as well as professionals, had to do their own. George Eastman, whose aim was to make photography a popular pastime, launched his Brownie box cameras in London and Paris in the early 1900s. Having started his European labs in Harrow and Paris, Kodak was followed by a number of finishers whose founders had to learn their craft by reading the photographic journals. It is not surprising that standards were variable and this was accepted, as it was difficult to distinguish between the quality of D&P and the limitations of the films and inexpensive cameras of that time. On the other hand many German amateurs, for whom photography was a more serious hobby than that provided by the early film cameras, continued using glass plates, which produced superior quality and consequently they expected a first-class D&P service.

In the early years of the last century, most of the D&P for German amateurs was carried out by photo shops and this situation continued until the early 1950s. From the 1920s onwards, an excellent camera industry had sprung up producing roll film cameras but, perhaps more importantly, 35mm cameras, starting with the Leica. Most of the German cameras, especially the 35mm models, were considerably upmarket compared to Kodak's Brownies and the customers expected and got top-quality prints. By the early 1930s, the quality of film had improved sufficiently for its convenience to greatly outweigh any reduction in quality, compared with glass plates.

It was a legal requirement until early this century, for professional photographers, or for any one running such a business, to be a Fotographen Meister. There were a number of loop-holes in the law; for example, school and passport photographers as well as those offering a D&P service were excluded. Nevertheless, the idea that any photo-related business should be run by a Meister was seen as a sign of quality, which many photo shops, some of which had a photo studio, almost certainly emphasised.

In addition to photo shops there were many Foto Drogerien, which were mini-markets selling films, as well as a few other photo products, cosmetics, toiletries and household items. Some did their own D&P, but others sent out the work. There were photofinishers in the 1920s and 30s, but probably not very many according to Rainer Heinze, whose father started his finishing business in 1931 in Breslau, now part of Poland. The family lost the business during the war and in 1952 started again in the Ruhr, but more of that later.

In 1936 Agfa released a colour reversal film followed by a somewhat improved version two years later. These were sold process-paid, the processing being carried out in Agfa's lab in Berlin. Kodachrome was also available in Germany but had to be sent abroad for processing.

At the end of World War 2, much of normal life had come to a standstill. However, there was a strong will to rebuild the country. Within a few years films again became available in West Germany and the finishing industry restarted. The situation in the eastern part was rather different in that many of the factories were dismantled and carried off to Russia and, due to the state of the economy, photography as a hobby remained much less advanced until after the reunification in 1990.

For the first decade after the war, nearly all photography was black and white and most finishing was still carried out by photo shops. As colour films and papers became available, it soon became clear that photo shops were not suitable for processing them and in the early 1950s specialist colour labs and finishers doing black and white as well as colour, were founded. Very few still exist as independent businesses, most having joined one of the few remaining groups.

The Largest Independent to Survive well into the 21st Century

The most successful German photofinisher during the last half-century had its origins in Oldenburg in northern Germany. This was the home of Carl and Helene Wöltje's photo business, a shop with a portrait studio, which, as usual, did D&P. In 1947 Heinz Neumüller, having recently returned from war service and needing a photo for a job application, went there to have his picture taken. The photographer was Sigrid, the owners' daughter, whom he subsequently married. The following year he became a partner in the business and the young couple set about building Europe's largest independent photofinisher.

Materials were still in short supply and it was some time until colour film and paper became available. Foto Wöltje became very active and built up a colour processing business to complement its existing black and white D&P. Initially this was for professional photographers but gradually amateurs were catered for.

The first colour films to become available were from Agfa, who also produced some of the processing equipment. Foto Wöltje's colour department opened in 1951 using Agfa Varioscop colour enlargers and hand processing. A year later they installed their first sheet-paper processing machine with a capacity of 6000 prints per day. For the next few years there was rapid expansion of the colour facilities, both in volume and additional processes as they became available. Heinz Neumüller, from early on, equipped his lab with the most modern machinery available and by 1961 they had installed the first Agfa colour printers as well as film and roll paper processors.

When the colour materials were first released the price of a 120 roll film was DM 7.20, by 1951 it was DM 5.85, nine years later it had dropped to DM 3.45 and in 1965 to DM 2.90. No doubt the latter prices were dictated by Kodak film imported from the USA. Similarly, the first colour prints, the size of "world postcards" (10.4 x 14.8 cm), were sold for DM 4.50. The high cost of colour prints, not to mention the often disappointing results, made some German finishers advise their customers to have B&W prints made from most of the negatives and order just a few colour prints from the best. The Agfa colour negative film of that time was very suitable for making B&W prints as it did not have the orange mask, now standard for all colour negative films. This was only a passing phase as the quality of the films soon improved and prices dropped.

For most of the 1950s, lower cost and better colour rendering meant that transparencies were much more popular than prints. This, of course, changed over the years as print quality improved and prices dropped. Transparency processing was initially reserved for a few Agfa designated labs and a similar situation existed for other makes. Agfa discovered that this brought them into conflict with many of their customers and they soon abandoned this idea. In contrast to Kodak and later Fuji, Agfa did not run their own finishing businesses and instead concentrated on selling their films, paper, chemicals and equipment. There must have been many instances when they were able to control photofinishers, without having to own and manage them.

Foto Wöltje specialised in colour prints and did not start processing transparencies until 1965. In 1961 they adopted a very distinctive name for their finishing business based on the initials of the founder Carl Wöltje. CeWe Color quickly became a recognisable brand and is now present in large parts of Europe. The introduction of Kodak's 126 Instamatic film in 1964, gave a big spurt to the colour business and in 1965 they opened a new, purpose-built, 4,000 square metre lab in a suburb of Oldenburg. Many observers thought the new lab was far too large, but Neumüller was vindicated when he ran out of space within a few years. Up until then the business had served local customers but was now extended to cover a wider area. Seven years later he doubled the size of the lab in Oldenburg and built a new lab in Munich.

During the 1960s and 1970s it continued to grow rapidly and with the availability of a succession of much improved colour printers from Agfa and several other manufacturers, productivity improved dramatically. Neumüller invested heavily in his labs both to achieve quality and in order to stay very cost-competitive.

CeWe Color was not the only photofinisher to start up in the 1950s and 60s. Other well known names, in no particular order, were Kiel Color, Foto Heinze, Koliphot, Nord Color, Fotocolor Wermbter, Foto Wegert in Berlin, Rhein Color, Foto Prien, Intercolor, Foto Annemie, Colibri, Foto Brunniger, Sud Color, V-Dia in Heidleberg, Allcopp, Uhlenhuth and of course Kodak who, in 1954, built a very sizeable lab adjacent to their head office and camera factory in Stuttgart. In addition, two large retail/mail order chains, Photo Porst and Foto Quelle opened their own photofinishing labs.

Most of these labs grew rapidly, both in volume of work as colour photography increased in popularity and also, perhaps more importantly, in capacity as colour printers became more productive. Black and white finishing in the 1950s and 60s was very profitable and many labs managed to invest in colour equipment. Also, first Gevaert and later Agfa, provided extended credit for their finisher customers. It is not surprising that the expansion of the labs was usually in advance of demand and this triggered both price reductions and mergers.

CeWe was very efficient and highly cost-competitive. It reduced its prices in 1967 and this put pressure on some of the weaker labs. At the same time it formed links with various other groups. One of these was Union Color, a chain of labs, which it formed with Kiel Color and Foto Heinze. The aim was to acquire some of the less successful labs so as to reduce the competition. This arrangement did not last and Kiel Color and Heinze split, but CeWe did merge its business with Vereinigte Color lab of Hamburg. In the next few years they took over a number of other labs including Nord Color and Koliphot.

Heinze

One of the earliest success stories was Foto Heinze, started as a black and white lab in Gelsingkirchen by the Heinze family in 1952. Growth, financed from profits, was rapid and they established a large customer base among department stores, drug stores and other non-traditional outlets, as well as photo shops who had decided not to do their own D&P. Initially, most black and white films had to be printed on sheet paper because of the need to use several contrast grades to obtain optimum results. This was a costly method, but prices were high, so this did not cause any serious problems. Soon they installed American Pako roll paper printers and these increased productivity dramatically. The snag was that they could only print on one grade of paper, which meant that some prints, particularly those from over and under-exposed negatives, were not as good as they might have been. Heinze introduced a machine printing service for their more price conscious outlets, where this was acceptable. This quality limitation did not last very long, as first Müllersohn and later Agfa introduced printers which could alter the contrast of the paper by pre-flashing – see Chapter 3.

As we have seen, Heinze had tried to co-operate with Neumüller but this did not work. Both were visionaries and very strong characters but, as is often the case, had different ideas on how to proceed. Heinze went into partnership with Kiel Color in 1977 but this came to an end when Herr Prien, the founder, died shortly afterwards.

Heinze was very ambitious and established six large labs to cover the whole of West Germany. During the 1970s and early 1980s it was a matter of opinion whether his labs or those of CeWe were the largest. He also believed that the Spanish market would grow in sophistication, similar to that of the northern European countries, and opened 12 labs in Spain, albeit that they were very much smaller than his German labs. At its peak, the Heinze Photo Group had a turnover of DM 120 million, employing about 1500 staff in Germany and another 500 in Spain. In an attempt to protect their prices, they established a brand name "Bilderland" but this was not very successful, as it was probably somewhat before its time. It turned out to be a very costly exercise, which contributed to the group's financial difficulties later on. For many years Heinze had been able to finance his growth from profits and thereby remained free to choose the suppliers for his paper, chemicals and equipment, which represent the major outgoings of any lab. When, in the late 1970s, this was no longer possible, he turned to Agfa for assistance. They gave him very generous credits, 180 days for paper and chemicals and probably longer for equipment.

In the early 1980s there was considerable over-capacity in the German finishing industry resulting in further price reductions. Heinze became financially stretched and was forced into receivership. The business closed in 1983, but the family managed to retain Thiele, a school photography business.

CeWe

CeWe retained its independence and became ever more competitive. It continued to grow, acquiring, opening or expanding labs in Germany and from the early 1970s, doing business in adjoining countries. Initially this was through their German labs but later on they acquired or opened labs in other countries, particularly France. By 1975, 20% of their business was in export. When the amalgamation of East and West Germany took place in 1990, they had just completed building a lab in Berlin and that made it easy to supply the new market. They followed this up with a lab in Dresden and, over the next few years, by labs in several of the east European countries.

In 1993 the CeWe group went public to help fund its continued expansion. By the early part of this century the group were employing about 4000 people and sales had risen to over €400 million with Germany accounting for less than half.

CeWe has been involved in a number of interesting projects. In the 1980s they spotted that there would be a considerable reduction in the time it took to produce colour prints if the printer and processor were coupled. This is of considerable importance when offering a same-day or overnight service. Their engineering department designed and prototyped a processor that could be coupled to a printer and this eventually became the Agfa VSP, variable speed processor. This has been very successful in conjunction with Agfa's MSP and Dymax printers.

In more recent years they have been very successful in their digital services. In particular, they have offered a "digital negative" to digital camera users. Many of CeWe's dealers are equipped with kiosks where the customer can burn a CD from his memory card. The CD cannot be accessed until the pictures have been printed by CeWe, after which it is "unlocked" before being returned to the customer, together with his prints. It can then be used for archiving, sending pictures by e-mail or printing on a home computer.

V-Dia

Willy Vogt who, pre-war, had been a photodealer in eastern Germany, in 1949 founded V-Dia in Heidleberg. Cinemas, showing mainly Hollywood films, had become popular and he had spotted a demand for advertising slides to be projected before the program. He quickly followed these with slide sets sold in resorts, often with the mounts printed with advertising matter. A few years later he added large colour prints for commercial use.

In 1965, Willy Vogt's son in law Siegfried Kube joined the business. Kube had a good schooling in colour finishing having worked in Agfa's application lab in Leverkusen under Dr. Heinz Berger, who was known in Germany as the "high priest" of colour photography. He also worked for Berkeycolor in New York where high-volume production of colour prints was more advanced than in Germany. Kube started a highly mechanised amateur film department to operate alongside the much more manual professional business.

All parts of V-Dia grew rapidly, equipped with the most modern machines and with a reputation for the highest quality. In addition to expansion in Heidelberg they acquired three more labs in the 1970s and, after the unification of Germany, opened several labs in the eastern part. V-Dia differed a little from the other German finishers in that their professional work was always a very important part of the business, whereas for most of the others it was a minor activity. From the early 1990s, they introduced digital imaging services.

By 2003 there were rumours that they had overextended themselves and the company, together with the Wegert lab in Berlin, was bought by a finance company, BHG Color and Print.

The Rise and Fall of Kodak Photofinishing

As we have seen, Kodak's serious entry into German photofinishing occurred in 1954 when they built a lab adjacent to their camera factory in Stuttgart. Initially its purpose was to provide processing for Ektachrome and Kodachrome transparencies, both still and 8 mm and 16 mm movie films. For many years the latter was a very major activity but this declined after the abrupt end to the sale of movie cameras with the arrival of camcorders.

35 mm transparency films became less important over the years but their market share in Germany has always remained a little higher than in most other countries.

In the 1990s, 35 mm Kodachrome film became a very small market for the enthusiast, as the quality of the more convenient Ektachrome and Fujichrome films improved. In January 2002 Kodak finally discontinued Kodachrome processing in Germany, but continued to send the few remaining films to be processed to Lausanne, Switzerland.

In the 1960s Kodak stepped up their photofinishing activities, introducing colour printing services, but the big growth came at the end of the 1980s when they took over Foto Annemie, Copaphot and Colibri. These were very successful companies and independent photofinishers welcomed Kodak, assuming that the purpose of the acquisitions was to demonstrate the high quality that was obtainable with

Kodak materials. During the next decade there were further acquisitions and by the Millennium, Kodak was operating 10 labs employing about 1400 people. Competition became very intense and this caused difficulties, made worse by the decline in film sales from 2001 onwards. Various attempts were made to stimulate sales by offering premium quality prints but these were only partially successful.

In November 2003 it was announced that Kodak had sold its German labs to BHG, making it one of the three large labs groups claiming about 25% of the market. At this stage BHG had 15 labs but, due to overlap and decline in the number of films, six of these were due for closure in 2004.

Fuji

Fuji's entry into German photofinishing, as in France, was to support their Single 8 movie film, initially with a lab in Willich and later a second lab in Ansbach. From the mid 1970s, as in the rest of Europe, Fuji were selling increasing amounts of colour paper and chemicals and for some years appeared anxious not to compete with their photofinisher customers and thus did not get into photofinishing in a serious way. The situation changed when Kodak began to expand their finishing operations, which threatened to squeeze out Fuji. In 1997 Kiel Color with two labs and Brunniger with its five labs, merged to form Eurocolor and in August of that year Fuji took a 75% stake in the business and it was eventually merged with Fuji's own labs. By 2003 Eurocolor was believed to be the second largest group after CeWe and was processing some 35 million films and making 1.3 billion prints per annum.

A few months after having acquired the Kodak labs, BHG went out of business leaving CeWe and Fuji to share the German wholesale photofinisher business between them.

It is interesting that, in Germany, minilabs have a much smaller share of the market than in most of the other European countries. It probably stems from the high quality demanded, which for a long time was difficult to achieve in a retail environment and certainly only at very high cost. Irrespective of cost, a minilab needs a skilled person to set it up, keep it calibrated and to correct prints from difficult negatives. It has taken many years for digital minilabs, with their very sophisticated software, to ease this problem. Many of the Grosslabor, as the wholesale finishers are called, are very cost-effective and have for many years offered a same-day service in the larger towns and that has limited the minilabs to those who really want a half-hour or one-hour service.

CHAPTER 11

Japan

By the Millennium, Japan was the second largest user of films after the US. However, this had not been the case in the first half of the 20th century. Photography had been on a fairly small scale with most films imported until the 1930s. Konishiroku started producing films in 1929 and Fuji followed in the mid 1930s but not too much is known about Japanese photofinishing at that time. Developing and printing was most probably done by photo shops and some of these had a number of branches. One of these was F Chartan Co. Ltd. founded in 1929 to export photo equipment. In 1935 they set up a chain of shops under the name APS, Amateur Film Service, to develop and print films. By 1937 they were building their own equipment for their labs. They had 25 branches in Osaka and 27 in Tokyo and were the first to offer a one-day service. They had a total of 100 staff, which does not suggest that they did work for other shops.

They processed Sakura and Fuji Pan 120 roll films, some glass plates and a few 135 and 127 films. We are told that their prices were about half the then-current rates. Prices quoted are:

Developing	
120 films	0.15-0.20 Yen (about US 4-6 cents)
135 films	0.4 – 0.5 Yen
Printing	
M size (118mm x 163mm)	0.1 Yen (about US 3 cents)
Card size (81mm x 106mm)	0.07 Yen
Business card size (65mm x 90mm)	0.05 Yen
Hand colouring of prints	0.5 Yen

We are told that, at that time, the Japanese prime minister earned 115 Yen per week, while the starting salary of a clerk in a major bank was 17 Yen per week.

The shops were all destroyed by air raids in 1944 but they restarted in Osaka In 1945. In 1952 they discontinued the processing business to concentrate on manufacturing equipment, a range of processors, and other photofinishing equipment, which is still carried out to this day under the name of FC Manufacturing.

The major developments in the photofinishing industry took place some years later.

Earlier in the century there had been a number of companies manufacturing cameras and they soon got going again in the early 1950s. The majority were unknown outside Japan. However, this was the period when names such as Canon, Nikon, Fuji, Asahi, Konica, Olympus, Mamiya and Minolta emerged. As the reconstruction of Japan after World War 2 progressed, photography quickly became a popular pastime. It no doubt suited the culture, not to mention that it fitted in with a rapidly growing economy. There were plenty of photo shops and these also developed and printed black and white films.

Colour reversal films became available in small numbers by the end of the 1940s and the manufacturers, Fuji, Sakura, plus Agfa and Kodak, set up labs to process them. Colour negative films arrived a little later, Agfa from 1954 followed by Sakura, Oriental, Mitsubishi, Kodak and Fuji in 1958. Agfa and Kodak were able to bring in their own processing machinery, but the others used mainly locally produced equipment. At that time there were no Japanese automatic colour printers, such as existed in the US and Europe, and consequently the prints were made using enlargers, which was a very slow and costly process. For a few years none of the Japanese manufacturers had a predominant market share, but this changed shortly afterwards.

The Japanese government, to protect its own industry, restricted imports of colour films to between 5% and 10% of the total market, effectively excluding Kodak and Agfa. Shortly after Fuji launched their colour negative film, they took on the distribution of Pako processing equipment and used this for their two large labs in Tokyo and Osaka. The Pako equipment was fairly expensive by Japanese standards and also needed a considerable amount of technical support and Fuji realised that these Pako equipped labs would only partially meet their aims to capture a large market share. In 1962 Fuji scoured the world for other colour printers and took exclusive agencies for all the available brands. These were the UK Colortron printers, those produced by Müllersohn in Germany and the French Priox printers. After a very thorough evaluation, they decided to adopt the Colortron printers for their chain of small labs throughout Japan. The choice of the Colortron printer was made because of its robustness and the fact that at the time it was far more stable than any other, including Pako. It was a high correction additive printer, which was very suitable for the early, unmasked Fuji colour negatives. During the next three years, Fuji opened 105 small labs, each equipped with two Colortron printers and, together with their two large labs, provided an excellent developing and printing service all over Japan.

As a consequence of Fuji having secured exclusive rights to all available automatic colour printers, Konica and Oriental Photo were unable to provide an effective processing service. Within a short time Fuji had more than 60% of the colour film and print market, most of which it has held onto ever since.

These Fuji labs provide an interesting insight into the state of the Japanese photo market in the early sixties and the means that Fuji used to become a very serious player on the world market later on. The two labs in Tokyo and Osaka appeared to be similar to large labs in the US or Europe, using Pako equipment. The small labs were rather different. In the first place, both films and paper were hand-processed in spirals. This gives an indication of Japanese labour and machinery costs relative to those in the US and Europe. However, the biggest difference appeared to be the attention to detail in order to maximise output from the printers and to ensure that the quality of the prints were the best that could be obtained from the film and paper. Each printer had two operators sitting side by side, one to pre-grade the negatives for subject failures, the other to feed the negatives with minimum interruption. The staff were highly trained by Fuji and the quality of the work seemed excellent, very much better and more consistent than that produced by most European small labs at that time. It is not surprising that colour prints became very popular in Japan at a time when many people in the West were complaining of the variable quality.

There were other indications of how Fuji and presumably other Japanese companies handled the photographic and in particular the photofinishing business. On several occasions the UK manufacturers of the Colortron printers submitted other equipment to Fuji. In each case they carried out a very detailed assessment and from their reports it seemed that they probably knew more about the equipment than the designer. The attention to detail was awesome and explains why over the following decades they improved the quality of their films and colour papers to make them world leaders. The ability to work like this was no doubt connected with the social system, which enabled the top Japanese companies to recruit and retain the educational elite. Very few US and European companies were able to match this and even Eastman Kodak, who in the 1960s and 70s had almost unlimited resources to spend on R&D, were unable to develop their products to the degree of consistency achieved by Fuji.

An interesting fact is that, by 1968, a prototype of the Yamatron colour printer named after its designer, Mr Yamada, was in use in one of the Fuji labs. It incorporated some interesting new features, but bore no resemblance to any US or European printers of that time. Whether it went into production is not known, nor were any exported to Europe. It must be assumed that Fuji were aiming for world-beating products and found that this was not too easy in the case of colour printers. It was many years later that a few Japanese printers, both Fuji and Sakura, appeared in the west and they were quickly withdrawn when it became apparent that they did not have much to offer compared to US and European printers. To this day, very few of the large labs use Japanese printers and many are equipped with Agfa MSP printers. The situation as regards minilabs, as we will see, is rather different.

The Noritsu company was founded in the early 1950s and its first product was a print washer followed by film processing machines. During the following two decades many of the colour print labs were equipped with Noritsu film and paper processors and a number appeared in Europe and the US. The machines were generally similar to those produced by US and European manufacturers but no doubt benefited from lower costs.

From this period in the sixties to the end of the 1970s there was a rapid growth in photography, particularly colour, and the photofinishing industry grew accordingly. By the middle of the 1960s half of all households owned a still camera and 10 years later that figure had reached close on 80%. In the same period the percentage of pictures taken in colour had risen from 5% to about 80%. Photofinishing volume had increased ten-fold but, due to the reduction in prices, expenditure had only grown four and a half times.

By the end of this period there were nearly 300 amateur photofinishers, some owned by, and the remainder affiliated to, one or other of the manufacturers. Only about 40% of these were in the Fuji stable, but nevertheless they dominated the market with a share of over 60%. This was in part due to the restrictions on Kodak and Agfa and, although these were eventually lifted, it remained extremely difficult for a foreign company to increase its sales.

Japan, due to its extremely efficient camera industry, was very much wedded to 35mm film and so the 126 Instamatic system which had been introduced by Kodak in 1963 did not become as popular as in other countries. However, the 110 pocket Instamatic introduced nine years later did catch on, probably because the small size of the cameras appealed to the youth and female markets.

Disc film and cameras, which were introduced by Kodak in 1982, were not a great success. The Japanese industry would not let Kodak use it to increase their market share. The fact that very few of the film and photofinishing outlets were controlled by Kodak made it almost impossible to establish. By then the accepted quality standards were beyond what disc cameras could offer and the widespread availability of autofocus 35mm cameras meant that disc cameras had little to offer other than size.

In 1976 Noritsu changed the way the photofinishing industry would look in the future. To be precise, this was not strictly true in the sense that the QSS-1 (Quick Service System1) was only the foretaste. The real thing came with the QSS-2 three years later. It was the first complete daylight-operating photofinishing system designed specifically for use in a retail shop. It was expensive and perhaps not quite as easy to use as the enthusiastic salesmen claimed, so initial take-up was fairly slow. Fuji, Sakura (Konica), Copal and Kodak soon followed Noritsu. In the first year, only about 30 were delivered but by 1981 this had increased to 200, with 500 in 1983 and 1400 in 1984. In that year, the minilab share of processing had reached close to 10%, which was much more than in other countries.

The continued growth of minilabs was quite spectacular.

Year	1985	1990	1995	2000
Number of minilabs	2100	12500	22500	27000
Market share	15%	35%	58%	70%

In the early part of this century the number of minilabs has declined, although the market share has not changed very much. This was due to the fact that newer minilabs tend to have a larger output and competition has forced many to work longer hours and so reduce costs.

Why should the market share be so much greater in Japan than in other developed markets? It is probably a combination of several reasons. On the one hand the wholesale labs are generally considerably smaller than in the US and Europe and hence their costs could well be higher, and this probably also applies to their distribution system. In the US and Europe the high costs of operating minilabs compared to the wholesales labs has limited the market share of the former. More of the Japanese minilabs are owned by small shopkeepers, who are willing to work the machines more intensely than in other countries and consequently charge a much smaller premium, compared to the wholesale labs. The situation is similar in other far eastern countries such as Thailand and, of course, China, where there are not many large labs.

Greeting cards with photos are very popular and these are sent in large numbers for the New Year. The business started in 1975 and in 1987 Fuji added a lottery ticket to the cards. The lottery ticket, complete with a stamp, is supplied by the post office and the labs laminate the customer's photo to the greeting card. In addition, the labs address the cards so that it makes a very convenient form of greeting, complete with a small present. Konica and Kodak offer a similar service.

In 1990 Olympus, followed by others, introduced 35 mm cameras with a facility for panoramic pictures. Photofinishers had no way of determining which frames had been exposed in the normal format and which were panoramic images. Initially this caused considerable problems and made automatic printing impossible.

At the 1991 Lab System Show several manufacturers, including Fuji, Noritsu and Konica, introduced minilabs, which could identify the different frames and allow semi-automatic printing. Eventually fully automatic printing facilities were added to most minilabs and also some high-speed printers such as the Agfa MSP. Panoramic formats caught on mainly in Japan and did not become popular in the rest of the world until after the introduction of the APS films and cameras in 1996.

The Japanese market was quick to take up new developments and the introduction of the APS system was no exception. Within one year of its introduction it had taken over 8% of the market share and four years later this had more than doubled. This was the first time that Japanese manufacturers, in particular Fuji, had been involved in the introduction of a major new film format and this, combined with the small camera sizes, was responsible for its rapid growth. The fact that the very popular panoramic format was available on all cameras must have been another reason for its popularity.

One of the most interesting phenomenon of the Japanese market is the growth of single-use cameras. They were introduced by Fuji in 1986 and most other manufacturers followed shortly afterwards. One million were sold in the first six months of introduction. In 1991 the name was changed to "Film with Lens" in order to raise their profile and emphasise that they were to be recycled. Two years later 55 million were sold and by 1996 the number had gone up to 80 million. Since then there has been no further increase and, in fact, since the Millennium sales have declined, dropping to about 70 million by 2003. However, this is a small part of the total film sales, which fell from 471 million in 1999 to 381 million rolls in 2002. One-time use cameras have, for some years, partly compensated for the decline in 35 mm and APS films since 1998. The popularity is largely attributed to high school girls for whom it became a craze. Interestingly the decline in one-time use cameras took place at a time when in other markets, such as the US and Europe, they were still increasing. This was probably due to the arrival of the next gadget, low-cost digital cameras.

Single-use cameras exist in various formats including 35 mm, 110 and APS. The latter is particularly popular in Japan, partly because of the panoramic facility which has at various times been heavily promoted, particularly by Fuji, in an effort to increase the number of APS films sold.

The fact that the first electronic still camera, the Sony Mavica, was a Japanese development probably influenced the move into digital photography. The Mavica in itself did not provide this, as it was an analogue camera based on TV technology and rather too complex and cumbersome for the "happy snapper". Its main effect was curiosity value and also to demonstrate that there were other methods of saving memories than film photography.

The Japanese have always been fascinated with gadgetry and so digital cameras found a ready market when they became available at affordable prices. The transition from film to digital cameras over the years has been quite dramatic.

Shipments of Film and Digital Cameras (Millions)

	1999	2000	2001	2002	2003	2004
Film type	4.18	3.58	3.02	2.24	1.15	0.62
Digital camera	1.5	2.95	4.83	6.55	8.44	8.55
Total	5.68	6.53	7.85	7.85	9.59	9.17

The sales of digital cameras were only levelling out by the end of 2005 and, with the decline in film cameras, it is not surprising that several manufacturers have discontinued them. As a consequence, there has been a very rapid drop in film sales.

Total Domestic Shipment of Roll Films (Millions)

1999	2000	2001	2002	2003	2004
470	460	431	371	310	250

One can assume that it will not be long before film sales become insignificant.

These changes have affected minilabs which have had to re-equip to cope with producing prints from digital cameras. The total volume of prints made by labs has dropped and this has resulted in intense competition.

Year	1999	2000	2001	2002	2003	2004
Total number of minilabs	26,563	26,990	27,123	26,300	24,280	22,015
Number of minilabs offering digital service	493	1,965	3,239	7,407	9,220	10,394
Digital lab %	1.9%	7.3%	11.9%	28.2%	38.0%	47.2%

The decline in film sales has similarly affected the wholesale labs. Between 1995 and 2005, labs belonging to members of the Japan Lab Association, decreased in number from 140 to 60. Now 80% of their work involves making prints from digital cameras and producing CDs. The total volume of prints produced is considerably less than at the Millennium.

The decline in film sales has been a challenge to the photofinishing industry and in particular to thc minilabs, with their large market share. As elsewhere the industry is working hard to persuade snap-shooters to print their images.

CHAPTER 12

Photo Labs and the Environment

Photofinishing, the developing and printing of films, involves chemical processes which generate considerable amounts of waste, not to mention the disposal of packaging materials such as film cartridges and cardboard boxes. Up to the 1960s very few people were concerned about the environmental effects of this and photofinishers dumped the chemicals into their drains, rivers or the sea and the solid waste into the dustbins (garbage cans). While business was good, very few labs tried to reclaim any of the waste.

As early as 1925 Eastman Kodak alerted US processors to the value of the silver, which could be reclaimed from used fixing baths and Photo Developments, the predecessor of the PMA magazine, gave detailed descriptions of how this could be done.[1]

Things changed dramatically during the late 1960s, when in many countries, people became concerned about industrial pollution. This was almost certainly nothing to do with photo labs, as very few people knew how they operated. The concerns were raised by the large industrial, chemical and steel works, which made many places, like Pittsburgh in the US and the Ruhr in Germany, very unpleasant places. Laws controlling pollution caused by the emission of fumes and the disposal of waste, were introduced across the whole spectrum of industrial and chemical plants irrespective of how little or how much pollution they caused. This of course included photofinishers which were variously classified as chemical or industrial plants.

Colour processing took off in the 1960s and Kodak and Agfa supplied ready formulated packs of chemicals. These were fine for small labs, but large photofinishers, such as CeWe in Germany or Eastman Kodak and other large US labs realised that they could make considerable economies if they prepared their chemistry from raw materials. This was quite a complicated process and required each of the labs to employ several qualified chemists. The economies came about in several ways. Apart from the fact that raw chemicals bought in bulk were considerably less costly than the manufacturer's packs, it quickly became clear that, when a photographic developer is used up, only a few of the components are actually used. This meant that the used developer, instead of being put down the drain, could be reconstituted by replacing a few of the constituents. This is not quite as simple as it sounds and usually involves analysis and hence the need for chemists. This also applied to other solutions such as fixers, bleaches and bleach-fixes.

In a suitably large lab, the chemists could more than pay for themselves and when pollution regulations were introduced, they were well placed to implement them.

The effluent laws fell into three parts. The most important concerned silver and were based on some dubious science. Silver is very important to the photographic industry because silver halides, i.e., silver bromide, silver iodide and silver chloride, are the light-sensitive compounds which are the basis of all photographic films and papers. In black and white photography part of the silver, in the form of metallic silver, forms the image, but the remainder is removed in processing. In the case of colour, the silver halides act as an intermediate and all silver is completely removed in processing.

The importance of photography for the silver industry is shown by the graph of world consumption. In 1925, when photography was still quite small, Eastman Kodak was using about three and a half tons of silver per week, worth over $60,000. By 1988 49% of the world's silver production, worth about $140 million, was used by the photographic industry. By the early part of this century this had dropped to about one-third of total production. The remainder is used for jewellery, silverware, coins and for other industrial uses such as electronics. The drop in consumption by the photo industry is probably a combination of the decline in film and paper production plus the fact that manufacturers have been reducing the amount of silver in each film and print.

Mexico, Peru, Australia and China supply about half of all silver, whilst the rest comes from a large number of countries around the world.

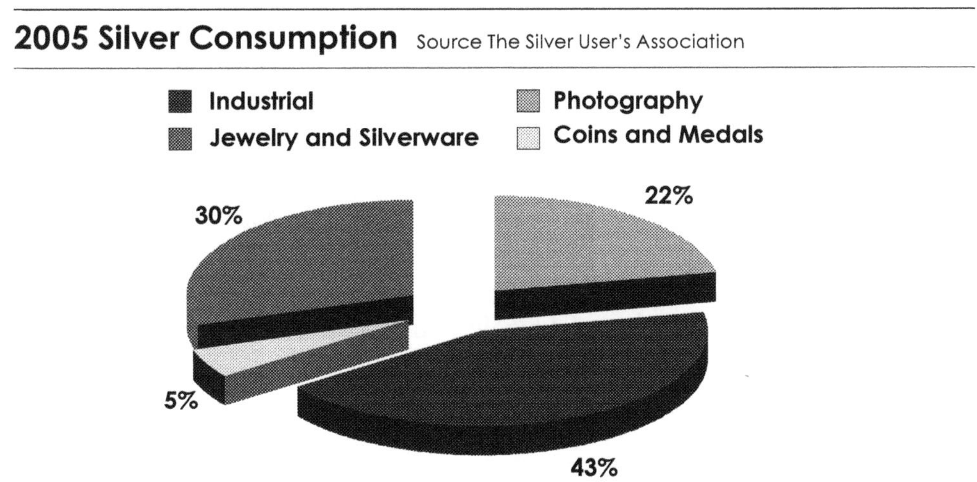

Silver – Science Misapplied

Silver exists in two forms. Silver and most of its compounds are non-reactive and if disposed of in reasonable quantities into drains or rivers will not harm fish or other wild life. In chemical reactions, such as those that take place in photo processing, silver compounds are in an "ionic" form and are extremely poisonous to humans and wildlife. In the course of the reaction, the silver compounds very quickly turn into their non-reactive form with the result that by the time the silver solutions reach the drains they are fairly harmless.

Unfortunately for the photo processing industry, many legislators assumed that most waste silver solutions are of the ionic form and hence fixed extremely low limits for the amount of silver permitted in waste streams. To see how unscientific this is, we have only to consider how pleased we are to use silver cutlery.

Eastman Kodak who, by the end of the 1960s, when these regulations started appearing, had an enormous research department working on all aspects of photography, should have known better about the toxicity of silver-bearing photo processing solutions. At that time they did not seem to take much interest in their customer's problems and made no attempt to lobby against these regulations. The photo labs probably did not understand the finer details of the processes and in any case were far too small to have any clout. Towards the end of the 1980s, the industry, backed by Kodak, formed the Silver Council to lobby the legislators, but it was too late. There are no uniform regulations and to get them changed would mean convincing literally thousands of different authorities all over the world, which was quite hopeless. The industry has had to accept them at considerable cost.

Some cynics might suggest that the chemists working in the large labs were quite happy to go along with these regulations which were difficult to implement, as it tended to make them even more indispensable. Companies that produced some of the silver recovery equipment had similar interests. That situation existed for many years until improved technology eased the situation.

It is relatively easy, and very cost-effective, to remove the bulk of the silver compounds from used photographic solutions and wash water, but much more difficult and costly to reduce them to the levels demanded by many authorities. It requires complicated equipment and highly trained staff but, from a health hazard point of view, it achieves very little.

Silver is not the only chemical getting into the waste stream, but it is the one that creates the most interest. Other substances include inorganic salts of sodium or potassium and ammonia-related compounds. While not desirable, most will decompose into substances which are found in nature and which are not poisonous in moderate quantities. There are others: sulphites, sulphates, phosphates and EDTA, many of which are found in food and drinks. There are also various iron compounds used in bleaches and the amounts discharged into waste are restricted in some countries.

Another form of pollutant are the organic compounds used in both black and white and colour developers. While they can be poisonous in waste water, if present in substantial quantities, their main problem is that they can cause dermatitis. Anyone so infected becomes very allergic to even small traces and has to give up handling photographic chemicals. Most photofinishers now require their chemical staff to wear protective clothes and gloves to reduce the chances of this happening.

In earlier processes, formaldehyde was widely used in film processing to harden the film emulsions so as to prevent them being damaged. This was considered to be carcinogenic and is also an irritant, with unpleasant fumes which can cause the eyes to water. Over the years the need for this has been reduced to minute quantities and so it is no longer a problem.

Whether justified or not, current effluent regulations have resulted in the industry collecting almost all – more than 99% and in some cases 100% – of its waste chemicals and having them taken away for treatment by government-approved waste handlers. What they do with them, or whether the problem is just moved from one place to another, is another matter. The photofinishing industry in the developed world is causing very little pollution, and its internal procedures and materials have eliminated most of the health risks seen in former times.

Until the late sixties, relatively few photofinishers in the western world – like the rest of the public – had much understanding of the environmental impact of their activities. Efforts to decrease their silver and other chemical waste were often non-existent. The industry did what most other industries did, they disposed of their exhausted chemical wastes by piping them directly into the sewer. As public treatment plants were very rare, most of this ended up in the water streams and coastal waters, sometimes even in lakes, where the public sewer system ended. Other industries did the same; smoke stacks were built to a height that would cause unpleasant fumes to leave the immediate environment and dilute themselves in the process, and waste landfills were converting estuaries into dry land on which houses were built. Today, our environment is suffering from the effects of this, but that is another story. Fortunately the photofinisher's wastes were much less hazardous than most others, and there was no air pollution coming from them, that is if one ignores the indirect effects of drawing on the public power supply, where the fossil-fuel power plants sent millions of tonnes of unpleasant things directly into the air.

So how did photofinishers move from a lack of concern for the environment to where we are now at the beginning of the 21st century?

Some time in the 1960s the majority of photofinishers became alerted to the fact that the silver they were pouring down the drains was actually worth good money, and hence the first attempt to reduce the amount of silver wasted, was to recover it. Many photofinishers were still hesitant – they were unfamiliar with the technology required and as it was in the heyday of a rapidly growing industry, the potential return per attention hour was thought to be much bigger if a manager tended to his production rather than spending his time playing with such alien activities as electrolysis, ion exchange and metal replacement. But slowly, through the combined effects of enlightenment, pressure from junior employees and persistent calls from manufacturers of electrolytic equipment, who saw a new potential market, silver recovery equipment found its way into the photo processing plants.

At that time every square metre of colour paper held between 1.2 and 1.6 grams of silver, all of which had to be removed during processing. Likewise, every colour negative film would contain between 0.2 and 0.5 grams of silver – also unwanted in the final product. For competitive reasons, the film and paper manufacturers were reluctant to release this information but, nevertheless, it became known and Kodak was probably the first to publish "ranges" of silver contents in their films and papers. The amounts varied with different products and have decreased somewhat over the years. Once this became common knowledge, the magnitude of the potentially recoverable silver and its value was better known.

A photofinisher who took in one million rolls of film per annum, a number that many, particularly in the US, achieved at that time, would on average also use about half a million square metres of paper and during processing would remove of the order of 750 kg of silver. At the beginning of the 1970s, silver was worth about $150 per kg, so that recovering this was worth over $100,000, quite a considerable sum.

The regulations also had their effect and photofinishers started to install electrolytic recovery equipment. In principle it is fairly simple, consisting of just a tank into which the silver bearing solutions are pumped and a carbon and a stainless steel electrode which are connected to a low voltage DC electrical supply. As the current is passed through the solution, silver is deposited on the stainless steel electrode. It does not adhere strongly and periodically it is peeled off and sold to a silver refiner. In practice, it is not quite so simple, some of the equipment is quite complicated and to work satisfactorily, some analysis and chemical adjustment of the solutions is required.

A problem with this kind of equipment is that it will remove about 80% of the silver, still leaving a concentration of 1–2 grams per litre in the waste solutions. This was far too much to meet the regulations in many places, where levels as low as 0.5 mg per litre were required. To achieve this, additional equipment, which was quite complex to control, was required.

At first, photofinishers settled for the easy part of recovering the bulk of the silver by electrolysis and either hoped that no one would notice the rest passing into the sewers, or sometimes diluted the remainder with fresh water, which–while meeting the regulations – did not actually reduce the amount of silver going to waste.

Then, something strange happened in 1980. The price of silver suddenly went through the roof. The three Hunt brothers from a Texan family in the oil business, cornered a large part of the silver market, driving the price up about ten-fold. This carried on for several years until the early 1980s when the price dropped sharply to somewhere above its previous values. An account of what happened can be found on the website of a silver dealer www.gold-eagle.com/editorials_04/laborde012704.html.

Silver Price 1995-2005 Source - Silver Institute

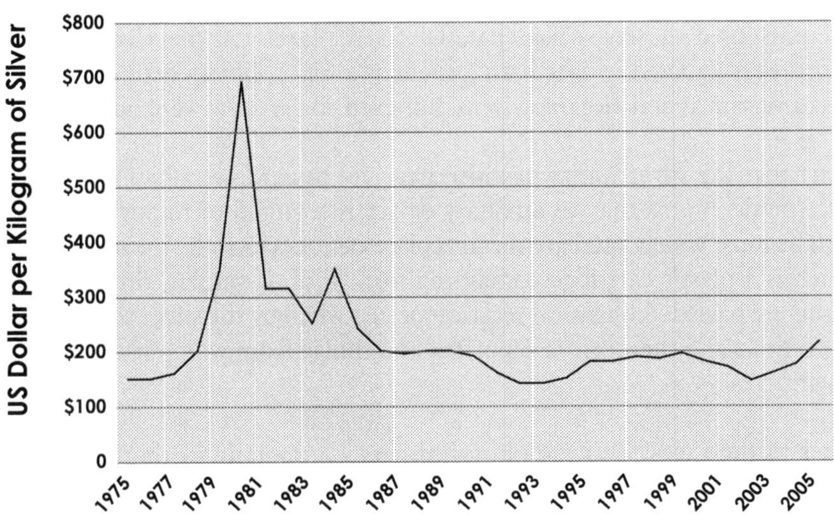

Apart from the regulatory requirements, the price rise of silver stimulated interest in silver recovery. Suddenly the value of the silver recovered from a roll of colour film and its prints had risen to as much as a dollar. Admittedly, this situation did not last for long. Many of the smaller photofinishers were privately owned and some decided not to sell the silver, but instead to keep it as a pension fund, which rather confirmed the old adage "investments can go down as well as up".

A number of greatly improved models of electrolytic recovery equipment were introduced, but these could only reduce the silver content of fixing or bleach-fixing solutions to about 0.2 g/litre, which was still several hundred times higher than that permitted in most countries.

For efficient electrolytic silver recovery, the solutions have to be agitated and several designs for this emerged. Most used fixed carbon anodes in close proximity with a circular stainless steel cathode, which was rotated by an electric motor. These were produced by many companies, including CPAC and Hallmark in the US, LED and Gregoris in Italy, and Agfa and Arnold and Richter In Germany. A rather unusual design was an Italian machine designed by an ex Kodak employee, Dr. Bellini. This used a row of vertically mounted carbon rods, which oscillated between stationary stainless steel plates. This claimed to require considerably less maintenance than the rotating electrode machines, which, due to the corrosive nature of some of the solutions, at least in the earlier days, required rather a lot of maintenance.

Hallmark in the US and Hauck in Germany adopted a completely different system. Their units used closely-spaced parallel fixed plates for the electrodes and the solutions were agitated by circulating them at a high velocity between the plates. It seemed a very neat and elegant system, but even so very few were built.

The fact that the silver limits in most areas are much lower than can be achieved by electrolysis, means that an auxiliary device is required to remove the remaining silver. The most widely used are metal replacement devices, the most common form of which is a plastic cartridge containing iron wool or similar, through which the solutions are passed. A chemical reaction occurs whereby the silver solutions become iron solutions and the silver is deposited as a sludge from which it can be recovered by smelting.

Another method used by large photofinishers, particularly in the USA, to recover silver from wash water involves adding a compound, which forms floccules with the silver and these are removed by filtration. The floccules are sent to a refiner who recovers the silver by smelting. The process was developed by Kodak using TMT, the flocculation agent produced by the German company Degussa. The first equipment was built by Kodak labs in the US. Later on Hallmark produced similar installations.

In several European countries, ion exchange equipment, not dissimilar to a domestic water softener, was used to remove silver and other impurities from the wash water. Suitably configured, the plant can remove all impurities so that the water is in fact recycled and can be reused. The silver is reclaimed by regenerating the columns from time to time. The system can work well, but requires skilled supervision and some labs, which were reliant on recycling all their polluted wash water, have found the system troublesome.

As the regulations have been tightened over the years, the position in many countries is that virtually no chemicals may be put down the drain. Most photo processes consist of a number of chemical steps followed by washing to remove chemicals from the film or paper. This means that, not only do the used chemicals have to be collected for haul away by a licensed waste company, but waste wash water has to have its chemicals removed before it can be put down the drain. As we have seen in this chapter this is not easy and certainly quite costly. Several technologies have evolved to deal with this.

Wash-less Processes

As we saw previously, minilabs replaced the wash part of the process with a chemical step called Super Stabilizer. Apart from removing the necessity for plumbed water and drainage in a retail location, this greatly reduced the amount of liquid requiring disposal. In most instances all the chemical overflows, including the super stabilizer, have to be collected and hauled away.

Some large photofinishers, especially in Europe, have opted for this method but its viability very much depends on the local regulations and facilities for meeting them.

Reduction of Chemical Waste and Wash-water Volumes

In the early 1970s over 300ml of chemicals and several litres of water, heated to about 25°C, were required to process one square metre of colour paper, the equivalent of about 60 amateur snapshots. This was not only quite costly but, to meet today's regulations, would require a substantial plant to clean the waste water. Since then there have been developments both in the chemistry and construction of the processing machines to make the process more economical and eco friendly. Today a little more than 100ml of chemicals and as little as 300ml of wash water would suffice to process the same amount of colour paper.

Chemical reduction has been achieved by recycling, whereby only those components that have been used up are replaced, or by an alternative technique where the chemicals have been reformulated so that much smaller quantities are required. Nowadays almost all labs mix or recycle their processing solutions using semi or fully automatic mixing machines. These are of two types. Large batch mixers, typically 500–2000 litres, which are used in Germany and a few surrounding countries, where many labs have traditionally employed chemists to analyse and adjust the processing solutions. In the US, Japan and the rest of Europe, small batch mixers, typically mixing 4½ litres at a time, are almost exclusively used.[2] These run unattended day and night and it is very rare for any chemical adjustments to be made.

Wash-water consumption has been reduced by splitting the wash into two sections. The first, called the "low-flow wash" uses only a very small amount of water, metered in proportion to the film or paper being processed. This section removes the bulk of the chemicals and this has to be collected with the chemicals for haul away by a waste company. The second part, usually called the main wash, has a somewhat larger flow, and removes the remaining chemicals from the film or paper. In some locations the chemicals trapped in the main wash are below the limits allowed to be put into the drains, while in others the water requires further treatment by ion exchange or flocculation.

To achieve these low rates of chemical and water usage, the processors have to limit the amount of liquid passed from one tank to the next. This is usually done by fitting squeegees, which remove the liquid from the surface of the strands of film or paper as they pass from tank to tank. In principle, they are similar to a motor car windscreen wiper blade, but of course in practice they are somewhat more sophisticated.

To achieve the low rates of wash water, the low-flow and main-wash stages are split into several tanks, the water cascading from one tank to the next in a direction opposite to the movement of the film or paper. The more cascading tanks there are, the less water is required, but there are practical limits to how little water can be used.

Reducing the quantities of chemicals and wash water has made the operation of a processor much more critical. Any slight variation in the performance of the replenishment system or the efficiency of the squeegees can have disastrous consequences. Modern processing machines, properly maintained, are essential, as is careful supervision.

Roll Paper Processor

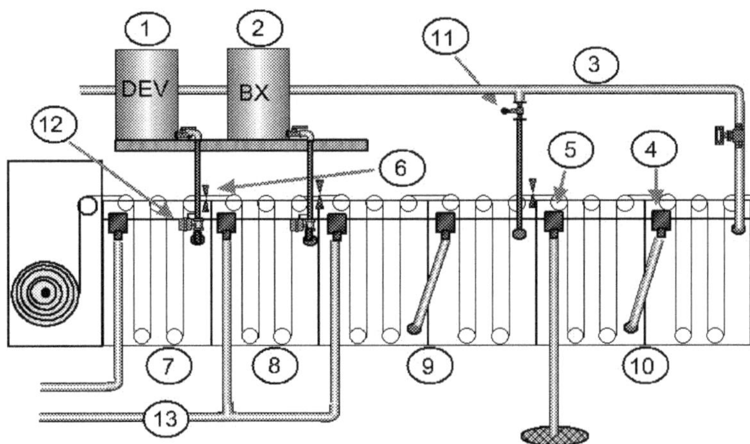

1 Developer replenisher tank
2 Bleach Fix replenisher tank
3 Water supply mains
4 Overflow box in main wash, with cascade pipe to previous tank
5 Overflow box from main wash tank with pipe leading to sewer
6 One of three sets of squeegees
7 Developer tank
8 Bleach Fix tank
9 Two cascade coupled low flow wash tanks
10 Two cascade coupled main wash tanks
11 Water flow regulator for low flow wash
12 Replenishment control valve for processing solution (developer)
13 Return pipes for chemical overflow to collection, silver recovery and haul away

Reducing the quantities of chemicals and wash water has made the operation of a processor much more critical. Any slight variation in the performance of the replenishment system or the efficiency of the squeegees can have disastrous consequences. Modern processing machines, properly maintained, are essential, as is careful supervision.

Haul away of used chemicals is very expensive, of the order of US 20–40 cents per litre, so reducing the quantities to a minimum is very important especially in "Zero Effluent Labs" where nothing is put into the drains. A photofinishing laboratory produces up to half a litre of chemical waste per film processed and printed, so that waste disposal can be a serious cost, especially in the very competitive situation which has existed in many countries since the mid 1990s. A number of companies have produced evaporators which vacuum-distil the waste to reduce its volume by 60%–80%. A bonus is that the water produced is reasonably clean and can be reused for mixing the bleach or bleach fixes. These machines, produced by among other companies, LED in Italy, Calfran in the US, Hauck in Germany and Bjornkjer in Denmark, have had only mixed success. They tend to be quite expensive, both to acquire and operate and what is worse, with the exception of the Danish machine, have had a mixed reputation as regards reliability.

In addition to chemical waste, photofinishers also have to dispose of considerable quantities of packaging waste. The industry has a good record, in most cases the waste is carefully segregated by type and, wherever possible, recycled. Waste includes cartons, film cassettes, film backing papers, empty chemical containers and drums and, most importantly, single use cameras (SUC), parts of which are reclaimed and rebuilt into new cameras. Here there has been an interesting situation; Fuji cooperates with Kodak to collect all the camera parts from their photofinishers, and then sort and exchange them. Fuji holds some very basic patents and, again cooperating with their arch rival Kodak, have successfully stopped third parties, who tend to use inferior film, from using Fuji and Kodak parts to build recycled cameras.

Most of the solid waste is classified as non-hazardous and hence its handling in most countries is not restricted to licensed waste companies. An example of how officialdom finds it difficult not to make an ass of itself exists in several countries. A full, sealed drum or plastic bottle of processing chemicals is classified as non-hazardous and can be transported without restriction even in a private car or taxi. However, if the container is empty, it is classified as hazardous, unless it has been washed to remove all traces of chemicals. The irony of this is that the water used for washing the containers becomes contaminated and cannot be put into the drains and has to be hauled away by a waste contractor. Most large labs purchase their processing chemicals in 60 or 200 litre drums, which are returned to the suppliers who clean and reuse them. This has led to the development of special drum washers, which will wash these drums using the absolute minimum of water. [3]

Monitoring

With strict rules on effluent disposal in force in most developed countries, the onus is usually on the labs to prove to the authorities that they are complying with the regulations or else face the prospect of heavy fines and/or losing their licence to trade. Analysis of waste water in order to measure silver content of the order of ½ – 5 parts per million, requires costly equipment and skills which are not available in every lab and so the task is often contracted out to specialists. In some countries the authorities make the labs install autosamplers in the drain, which take a small sample every hour and these are then mixed together and an average is analysed either daily or weekly. It is a costly procedure for the lab.

A few labs are using an effluent monitor, which works on an entirely different principle. Sensors are installed in the wash tanks of all the processing machines and these measure the amount of chemicals in the wash tanks by comparing the conductivity of the polluted wash water with that of the fresh water. They use these to compute the amount of silver and other pollutants flowing to the drains. It is an altogether simpler system than chemical analysis but, more importantly, gives immediate warning if, through a machine fault, the contamination level has increased. [4]

The Future

In the first decade of this century, the use of film for picture taking is declining rapidly and the photofinishing industry is concerned more and more with making CDs calendars, photo books and other gift items personalized with pictures. In addition to silver halide, an increasing proportion of prints are made by ink-jet printing so that the environmental situation is shifting more and more towards packaging, not forgetting the industrial processes used to provide the inks, papers and other material.

1 Photo Developments 1925, Page 41
2 See Automatic Chemical Mixers www.rockwellhitec.co.uk
3 See Drumwash www.rockwellhitec.co.uk
4 See Effluent Monitor www.rockwellhitec.co.uk

POSTSCRIPT

The Rest of the World

This book consists of a short history of amateur photography, a description of the technology of photofinishing, together with an account of its development in six countries.

There are of course many other countries which have a long and distinguished history of photofinishing. Due to the size of the countries, or the economic situation for much of the time covered by this book, the photofinishing industries in those countries have been much smaller than those we have described.

It would be very wrong in any history of photofinishing to ignore the many innovations that have come from these countries. While the same basic technologies are used in all the developed world, many photofinishers in the smaller markets have developed their own methods to provide an efficient service.

We have not written about China and India, where photofinishing is growing rapidly, but this is fairly recent and is not yet history. Nor have we mentioned, except in passing, all the other countries which make up our planet, in most of which D&P has been available for a long time.

Computer Terminology

Digital image A series of electrical signals which can be used to produce a visual image by a number of different methods.

File size measurements

Bits Digital signal 0 or 1 in which data is stored.

Kb = Kilo bits Number of thousands of bits.

Mb = Mega bits Number of millions of bits.

Byte Data character (Alpha or numeric) consisting of 8 bits

KB = Kilo bytes Size of a file in thousands of Bytes.

MB = Mega bytes Size of a file in millions of Bytes.

B/s or Kb/s or Mb/s Speed of a file transfer - number bits/ second.

JPEG A compressed format for storing digital images.

Laser A light source used for printing digital images onto photographic paper.

Photo CD A Kodak innovation launched in 1992 consisting of a recordable CD together with some software to store up to 100 digital images in several image sizes.

TIFF A non-compressed format for storing digital images.

Films, Photographic Papers, Formats and Processes

APS Advanced Film System introduced by a consortium of companies in 1996.

C22 The Kodak process for developing colour negative film superseded by the C41 process.

C41 The Kodak process for developing colour negative films now adopted by most other manufacturers.

Colour negative film Colour film used for making prints.

Contact print Print made from negative in contact with printing paper.

Disc film Kodak film format introduced in 1982 .

E6 The Kodak process for Ektachrome colour transparency films now adopted by most other manufacturers.

Ektachrome Kodak's colour transparency or slide film.

Full frame 35 mm 36x24mm frames exposed along length of film.

Half frame 35 mm 24x18mm frames exposed across 35 mm film.

Instamatic films 126 and 110 cartridge film systems Introduced by Kodak in 1963 and 1972.

Kodachrome The first really successful colour transparency process introduced by Kodak in 1935.

Orthochromatic films and papers Sensitive to Blue & Green light. They can be processed under yellow or orange safelights.

Panchromatic films and papers Sensitive to Blue, Green & Red light. They have better colour response than orthochromatic, but need to be processed in the dark.

Printon Ansco material on a white plastic base for making prints from transparencies.

R3 The Kodak process and colour reversal paper used for making prints from transparency or slide films.

Slide film Colour transparency film.

Photo Lab Equipment

Colour printer Machine which exposes photographic colour paper, usually from colour negatives.

Continuous or cine type film processor Machine for processing long rolls of spliced together films.

Digital colour printer Machine which exposes photographic colour paper from digital images.

Dip and dunk processor Machine for processing films by sequentially placing them in a series of tanks containing the processing solutions and wash water. Also called Rack and tank, or hanger processor.

Dymax Agfa colour printer developed from the MSP which corrected for negatives containing both over and underexposed parts ie. Strong highlights and shadows.

Film scanner A device for producing digital files from films. Frequently used in conjunction with a digital minilab or high speed digital printer.

MSP Agfa colour printer released in the mid 1980s which solved the problem of printing different types of films by scanning the whole film to determine its printing characteristics.

Scanner A device for producing digital files from films or prints.

Splicer Machine for joining together individual films into long rolls for processing in a continuous film processor.

VSP Variable Speed Processor - the best known is the Agfa paper processor which couples to a colour printer.

Types of Processing Labs

D&P Developing and printing – The main service provided by photofinishers

Digital minilab A minilab which makes prints from digital files. Frequently includes a film scanner so as to be able to print films

Free standing minilab Retail Minilab not part of other another business.

Minilab Daylight machinery for processing and printing films, usually colour negatives. Most frequently, but not always, used in a retail environment.

On line photofinishing Printing of digital images received via the internet.

On site processor (OSP) A Minilab developing and printing in retail premises, usually a drugstore, supermarket or mass merchandiser.

Overnight processor Wholesale Photofinisher processing films overnight.

Photofinishing The business of developing and printing films. In recent years extended to include manipulation and printing of digital files and production of photo cards, books and other photo related gifts.

Wholesale photofinisher Photofinisher Supplying Retail Shops.

INDEX

L

M

N

O

P

Q

R

S

SPECIAL THANKS

We have been overwhelmed by the generous assistance we have received from so many people without whom this book would not be possible. Please accept our apologies if we have overlooked any names.

AlanAcres,DavidBarnes,JulianBaust,IanBennell,RichardBradley,HalBriscoe,SueBromfield, Mike Callaghan, Stan Carr, John Childs, Ray Clipsom, Tony Cornish, James Crawford, A F Dorman, Katherine Evans, Peter Fitzgerald, Ernie Gilburd, Reg Hardy, Keith Harris, Bill Holmes, Ron Houslip, Ralph Jacobson, Don Kennedy, Ravi Khanna, Tony Lawrence, Robert Leggat, Fred Lewis, Bob Mayson, Pierre Mueller, Vinod Patel, Charles Plant, Malcolm Pyrah, Chris Roberts, Martin Rowlands, Ian Tait, Jon Tarrant, Dennis Taylor, Ron Thompson, Robert Vallance, Anthony Ward, Ian Wareham,

Gordon Addington, Frank Baillergeon, Donald Becker, Tessie Bourdamis, Brent Boyer, Connie Briggs, Harry Carhart, Neil Cohen, Melvin S Cohen, George Crompton, Kevin Donohue,AlexDreyfoos,JimEsp,StephanieFisher,TedFox,DonFranz,JeanneGarment,Peter Krause,KenLassiter, TedMcGrath,GaryPageau,ThelateSiPavelle,ThelateRoyPung,JimRice, Milner Robinson, Bob Sentell, Herb Stein, Ron Wilson,

Bernard Alexandre, Claude Bloch, Pierre Charnier Alain Choquet, Marc Contet, Rebert Dattola, Jean-Yves David, Claude Develay, Philippe Gysel, Roger Hamelle, Tanneguy. de Poulpiquet, Caroline Poux, Bruno Renier, , Georges Rollet, Pierre Rosenblum, Henri Sallard,

Hella Hahm, Manfred Heim, Rainer Heinze, Ina Hilker, Marion Knoche, Gert Koshover, Gunther Post, Christian Prien, Friedhelm Roeder, Hübert Rothärmel, Wolfgang Sieber, Gerhard Walther, Johan Zauner,

Tullio Cagna, Jurgen Delfs, Michael Donaldson, Rino Fornari, Guilio Forte,

Shinji Arai, Michio Fujimoto, Yujii Igarashi, Yukihiko Matsumoto, Toshio Tsukada

Dutch Society of Photographic Collectors

This book has required an enormous amount of international cooperation which would have been considerably more difficult without email and high speed internet services.

We thank you all for your help, hopefully you will enjoy reading about our industry.

Peter Rockwell	Peter W Knaack
London	Copenhagen

The authors have spent most of their working life in the photofinishing industry and during this time witnessed a fascinating story unfold.

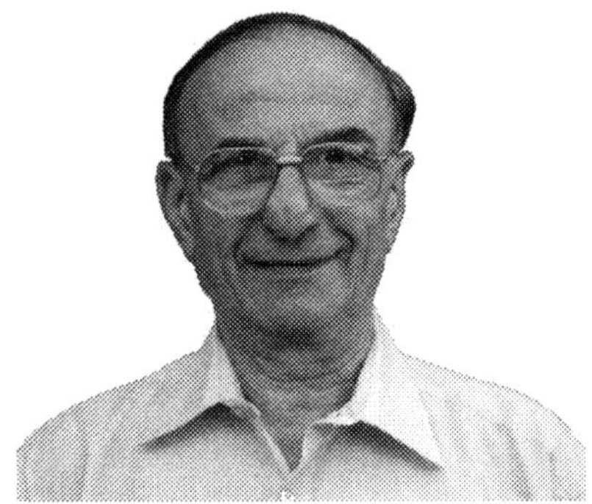

Peter Rockwell, an electronic engineer, entered the industry in 1961 and worked in design, production and marketing of photofinishing equipment. He has held senior positions in England with Pavelle, Kreonite, Propak Photographic Equipment and Rockwell Hitec, the market leader in photographic chemical mixing, which he founded in 1982.

Peter Knaack, a chemical engineer, entered the industry in 1972 and for 25 years worked In senior positions for Kodak's photofinishing businesses in a number of European countries.

During some years as an independent consultant advising labs in the USA and several European countries, he helped to set up one of the first large modern photofinishing labs in Russia.

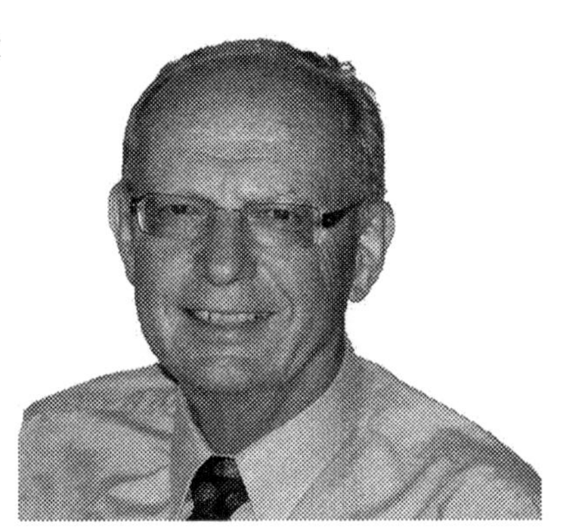

From early 2001 until recently, Peter has been Vice President of Operations of Shutterfly.com in California, one of the first successful digital online photo labs.

He now lives in Copenhagen.

Contact
Mr. Peter L.M.Rockwell
7a Courthouse Road
LONDON N12 7PH
UK Tel: ++44 (0)20 8445 3574 E-mail: prockwell@2ppress.com

www.ingramcontent.com/pod-product-compliance
Ingram Content Group UK Ltd.
Pitfield, Milton Keynes, MK11 3LW, UK
UKHW021046200726
13857UKWH00003B/852